great
potatoes

A Cook's Guide to Over 150 Delicious Recipes

kathleen sloan-mcintosh

VIKING
CANADA

VIKING CANADA

Published by the Penguin Group

Penguin Books, a division of Pearson Canada, 10 Alcorn Avenue, Toronto, Ontario, Canada M4V 3B2
Penguin Books Ltd, 80 Strand, London WC2R 0RL, England
Penguin Putnam Inc., 375 Hudson Street, New York, New York 10014, U.S.A.
Penguin Books Australia Ltd, 250 Camberwell Road, Camberwell, Victoria 3124, Australia
Penguin Books India (P) Ltd, 11, Community Centre, Panchsheel Park, New Delhi – 110 017, India
Penguin Books (NZ) Ltd, cnr Rosedale and Airborne Roads, Albany, Auckland 1310, New Zealand
Penguin Books (South Africa) (Pty) Ltd, 24 Sturdee Avenue, Rosebank 2196, South Africa

Penguin Books Ltd, Registered Offices: 80 Strand, London WC2R 0RL, England

First published 2002

10 9 8 7 6 5 4 3 2 1

Copyright © Kathleen Sloan-McIntosh, FoodPrint Inc., 2002

Interior photos: The DK Picture Library

Printed and bound in Canada on acid free paper ∞
Manufactured in Canada.

National Library of Canada Cataloguing in Publication Data

Sloan-McIntosh, Kathleen

    Great potatoes : a cook's guide to over 150 delicious recipes / Kathleen Sloan-McIntosh.

Includes index.
ISBN 0-670-04348-6

    1. Cookery (Potatoes) I. Title.

TX803.P8S67 2002   641.6'521   C2002-902732-2

ATTENTION: CORPORATIONS
Books are available at quantity discounts with bulk purchase for educational, business, or sales promotional use. For information, please email or write to: Penguin Books, 10 Alcorn Avenue, Suite 304, M4V 3B2. Email: lorraine.kelly@penguin.ca. Please supply: title of book, ISBN, quantity, how the book will be used, date needed.

Visit Penguin Books' website at **www.penguin.ca**

To Win & Mac,

with "a bushel and a peck"

of love and gratitude …

Pray for peace and grace and spiritual food,
For wisdom and guidance,
For all these things are good.
But don't forget the potatoes.

—Anonymous

Contents

Detailed Contents

The Comforting Potato 61

The Winter Potato 135

The International Potato 157

My Dad came from Belfast and it was he who taught me, through fine example, how to *really* eat potatoes—at any time of the day or night.

the potato
and I

In 1793 a certain Mme Meridiot was the first woman in France to publish a cookbook. Entitled *La cuisine républicaine,* it is entirely devoted to potato recipes. Try as I might, I haven't been able to get my hands on a copy, so I thought, well, it's about time another woman wrote a cookbook entirely devoted to potato recipes—and here it is.

You could say that this book is a logical outgrowth of my ongoing love affair with the potato. Mine is the most natural of passions, as each of my parents considered the potato to be a serious meal-maker. My Nottingham-born Mum started each and every dinner by ritualistically peeling the potatoes—it simply wasn't dinner without them. One of my earliest cooking memories is of trying in earnest to peel the supper potatoes as deftly as Mum. I would marvel at how she used her paring knife to remove just the thinnest layer of peel while I always took off far too much. These would have been older potatoes, as she called them, good for boiling, mashing or baking. When new potatoes were available, peeling became unnecessary, at least before boiling.

As for my Dad, well, he came from Belfast and it was he who taught me, through fine example, how to *really* eat potatoes—at any time of the day or night. Left-over boiled spuds were fried in the breakfast pan with sausages and bacon, or on Mondays, combined with leftover Sunday-dinner mashed turnip to have at lunch or as an after-school filler (a preparation the Scottish call *clapshot,* the traditional

1

accompaniment to haggis). We would even steal a couple of cold, left-from-dinner spuds out of the refrigerator late at night, treat them to a smear of butter and a little salt ("butter first so the salt sticks," Dad said) and devour them out of hand like apples.

Certainly, whenever the need for quick nourishment struck, one of his favourite dishes started with a salted lot of spuds being set to boil. Once cooked they would be coarsely broken up with a fork against the side of the pot, to which a few good lumps of butter and a handful of chopped green onion were added. This was *champ,* the comfort dish of Irish peasant origin he invariably enjoyed with an icy glass of buttermilk, as he had done as a boy in Ireland. I thought it was named for Dad, as he'd been a former featherweight boxer in Northern Ireland and still had the emerald green satin boxer shorts to prove it. When Mum felt he needed extra nourishment, she would nestle a halved, soft-boiled egg into the mound. A cold shard of butter would be set on it to melt, followed by a bit of salt and white pepper—always white pepper. I remember clambering up to sit on his knee where I would wait as he nudged torn bits of bread into the lovely warm yolk for me. But I kept my eyes on the prize—the floury bits of potato licked with butter—and invariably won some.

My beloved Uncle Bob, my Belfast-born godfather who was married to Auntie Madge, one of my mother's sisters, provided me with my most precious potato experiences. Visiting my five cousins on a Saturday meant staying for dinner. Staying for dinner generally meant watching old movies, too, late into the evening. Engrossed in the magical world of black-and-white film, we barely noticed Uncle Bob quietly leave his chair and head for the kitchen to make— glory of potato glories—potato bread. Not bread in the strict sense of the word, the potato bread he would make has an endless list of aliases: boxty, fadge, potato griddle cakes, potato scones, tatties or parleys and any number of other names. In this preparation, leftover mashed potatoes are combined with judicious amounts of butter and flour to make a dough. It requires deft handling, and just the right quantity of butter and flour before being roughly rolled out—not too thin, not too thick—cut into odd squarish shapes and fried in butter until speckled brown on each side. My uncle would pile the pieces on a plate and anoint them with a little more butter and a shake of salt before offering them to our waiting hands. How wonderful the potato bread smelled! And how it tasted!

Though I hardly knew it then, this simple preparation became my benchmark for every potato dish to follow, containing as it did everything about the potato I love. Earthy and comforting, potato bread held the very essence of potato flavour, and when it was gone, one longed for more.

That is my fondest potato memory, but I have so many more. Mum always cooked new potatoes whole, plunging a bunch of fresh mint into the boiling water along with a good bit of salt. The mint lent a very subtle influence to the potatoes, and the fragrance as they bubbled in the pot filled the air; something good was coming. Mashed potatoes in my childhood home were unfailingly perfect, created every time from scratch, by hand. They were lump free and, with those seemingly paradoxical qualities inherent in great mashed potatoes, at once fluffy and creamy.

Sometimes we just had boiled spuds that Mum would crush slightly with the back of a fork against the sides of the pot and serve with a bit of butter and maybe a little parsley. Baked potatoes were really baked potatoes. Never wrapped in foil, they were scrubbed and placed on the oven rack whenever we had meatloaf. Mum left them there until the exteriors were crackly. I stole the empty skins from everyone's plate. Roast potatoes on Sunday with the weekly roast beef and

Yorkshire pudding were crusted and sticky, slightly caramelized nubs that needed nothing, not even gravy, to make them better. Scalloped potatoes with a big, pink ham were the reason I rushed home from Sunday school at Easter. Then there were the chips—not French fries, mind you, but chips. At least once a week, potatoes were "chipped" and tumbled into the waiting reservoir of hot drippings that Mum collected throughout the week—no chips, fries or frites eaten anywhere since have ever come close. We might have them on a Saturday to accompany a little quick-fry steak; I would valiantly try to reserve a few to use as filler for a piece of white bread and butter—voilà, the chip butty. One weekend evening, to combat teen ennui, my dear Mum emerged from the kitchen with a bowl of homemade potato chips—saratogas, she rightly called them—just for me. Warm potato chips, shatteringly crisp with golden chewy edges. Everyone should have that once-in-a-lifetime experience.

Mum's first choice were King Edwards that, at that time, were grown in Ontario and P.E.I. These were big spuds with creamy flesh that she felt were without equal, originating as they did in the U.K. in the early 1900s. They remained her reliable favourite. Even many years later, when those yellow-fleshed Canadian tubers called Yukon Golds became the darlings of chefs and home cooks from one end of the country to the other, Mum, being suspect of anything new in the agricultural world, still maintained the superiority of a "good King Edward."

But the golden, world-renowned Yukon Gold was the impetus for this book. Like basketball and the Bloody Caesar, Joni Mitchell and Jim Carrey, the Yukon Gold potato—the superstar of the spud family—is all-Canadian in origin, brought to us and the rest of North America by Garnett Johnston, a world-class potato breeder. Before he died in 2000, Johnston received an honorary doctorate of science from the University of Guelph for his work there on breeding new potato cultivars.

Garnett told me that, when his European neighbours mentioned how much they missed the wonderful yellow potatoes they used to enjoy at home, he started researching the possibility of a variety that would take to Canadian soil: "I named it after a river—named all my potatoes after rivers. Got nothing to do with the Yukon other than that—just thought of the river and the gold rush." I asked him if it was popular due to its inherent versatility. "Don't know ... I think people like it because they can ask for it by name. Most people are not that familiar with other potato names, so they're not always sure what they're getting."

Maybe. I think timing had a lot to do with it. Precisely at a time when everyone turned fat phobic and butter suddenly became a four-letter word, the heavenly flesh of the Yukon Gold looked and tasted like forbidden fruit. Split open a baked Yukon Gold and it looks like it comes ready buttered. Because we eat with our eyes, it even *tastes* buttery.

As with so many of the good things in life, it all boils down to taste. And a good, fresh potato—of any variety—is nothing if not tasteful. This fact was truly brought home to me this past summer as I took part in our own little potato harvest. Unearthing dozens of flawless Yukon Gold potatoes from the black soil was the closest I have come to uncovering buried treasure. What a joyful thrill to lift them from the earth, wipe them clean, plunge them into boiling water and eat them tossed with butter and salt just a few moments later.

I hope my passion for potatoes and this collection of recipes will inspire you to grow a few of your own. Few things you can do for yourself and those you love will provide as much earthly pleasure.

No other vegetable—and few foods in general—incite culinary passion as resoundingly, as precisely as the potato. And no other vegetable has played such a significant role in history.

facts and myths, lore and legend

No other vegetable—and few foods in general—incite culinary passion as re-soundingly, as precisely as the potato. Since the Spaniards first brought it home from Peru in 1570, it has been feared and reviled, beloved, revered and relied on in equal measure.

And no other vegetable has played such a significant role in history as the potato. It has provided almost sole sustenance for millions, been presented at court in Europe and been grown high in the Andes and all over Ireland. At various times throughout history, potatoes have been used as entire army rations and hailed for their delicious properties by *haut(e)s* French chefs.

The Incas were the first to grow the potato as a serious crop some 8,000 feet (2,438 metres) up in the Andes. In the 1500s, Spanish explorers discovered the vegetable while searching for gold. And it is the Spanish pronunciation *batata*—for *papa* or *patata*, the word the Incas used for the sweet potato—that provided the English derivation. The sweet potato carries the name too, even though it is botanically unrelated to the potato.

Testimony as to how the potato was introduced to Europe varies, but it seems most likely that potatoes made the journey via Spanish ships, stuffed as an inter-esting oddity into the pockets of the sailors who manned them. Home gardeners, while they thought potatoes made a lovely ornamental addition to their gardens, were more than a little suspect of the tuber itself, especially since it belonged to the same family—Solanaceae—as the poisonous deadly nightshade, to which tobacco, tomatoes, sweet peppers and eggplant also belong.

This vegetable—which is now considered to be the most important vegetable crop in the world and the most vital and important food crop after rice, wheat and corn—started its Old World life in Europe as a humble, whimsical garden crop and eventually appeared in North America. The potato was a bit of a curiosity, planted mainly for its pretty ornamental foliage and little else. It has been reported that, in 1586, Sir Francis Drake brought more potatoes back to England, while Sir Walter Raleigh is said to have presented them at court to Elizabeth I and to have introduced them in Ireland. These theories, which are not supported by hard evidence, seem to be part of the legend and mystery that surround the spud. As the English tried to decide just what to make of the vegetable, Antoine-Auguste Parmentier, a French pharmacist and agriculturist who had spent time in a Westphalian prisoner of war camp, wrote a thesis singing the praises and virtues of the potato, the vegetable that had kept him alive while in prison. The Germans had decided that the *kartoffel,* as they called it, was a suspicious vegetable, fit only for prisoners and pigs. In fact, they held that a person could catch leprosy by eating potatoes, a belief that the thriving Parmentier obviously disproved. As well as opening soup kitchens to feed the poor, he worked relentlessly for 40 years to turn his countrymen on to the wonders of the potato. During that time he attracted the notice of Louis XV, who funded Parmentier's research and efforts to popularize the potato and encourage its cultivation. At one time Parmentier hosted a special evening for a select group of guests who enjoyed a 20-course dinner, each one consisting of a potato dish. Many of those dishes—which even now bear his name—are still enjoyed today.

As Parmentier extolled the potato's virtue, the Irish were discovering how well suited the potato was to their country's climate and soil. More than any other European country, Ireland embraced the potato, cultivating it extensively, as had the Incas before them, as a field crop and staple. Praties, as potatoes were called, were mainly the food of the poor in Ireland. Eventually potatoes at least partially replaced oats—on which the people had relied heavily—as a staple, especially during those years when the oat harvest was less than expected. The potato was unfussy; it didn't require wonderful soil conditions or special tools, and it absolutely thrived on rain, of which Ireland had plenty. Most important, the potato was nourishing. An average five-ounce (142 g) potato can supply half of the total daily requirement of vitamin C, moderate amounts of vitamin B_6 and considerable amounts of niacin, pantothenic acid, riboflavin and thiamin. The potato contains essential minerals—such as copper, iron, magnesium, potassium, phosphorus and zinc—just a trace of sodium, good complex carbohydrates and even protein. During the early 1800s, households across Ireland consumed on average about five pounds (2.3 kg) of potatoes per person a day; it constituted 80 percent of the diet of the Irish.

Other famines related to field crops caused hardship and death in Ireland, but nothing came close to the devastation wrought by the three-year blight of *Phytophthora infestans*. Although this deadly fungus struck all of Europe, it devastated Ireland with particular ferocity from one end of the country to the other. The potato blight ruined the entire plant—from root to tuber to leaf. The resulting Great Famine of 1845–49 was so incredibly widespread because many people grew the same cultivar of potato, farmers and home gardeners sharing seed potatoes and plants with each other. Such was the absolute potency of the blight that it affected every species of potato in Ireland. Before the famine, the population of Ireland was more than eight million. Almost a million and a half men, women and children died from starvation and related disease during the famine. At least another million people left Ireland during that time for North America, Australia and England. Over the next six decades, by the early 1900s, Ireland's population had fallen to a little over four million. So much and so many were affected by so humble a plant.

Today the potato is everybody's favourite vegetable, loved by farm families and five-star chefs alike. The varieties of potatoes are endless and include more than 400 catalogued species of white potatoes—the common variety that used to be called Irish potatoes—alone. Potatoes come in white, yellow, red, purple and lilac varieties and can be used for boiling, baking, roasting, mashing and frying. There are russets and long whites, round reds and oval whites. Potato lovers can enjoy potatoes of every shape, size, texture and colour throughout the year in an endless array of dishes.

In Canada we choose Russet Burbank or Russet Norkotah for roasting, baking or mashing, Yukon Golds for boiling or roasting (and really just about anything) and round reds like Chieftain or Rideau for salads and gratins.

the cultivated
potato

Potato varieties have come a long way since their initial discovery in the foothills of the Andes. Potatoes are serious business and the world's largest food crop after rice, wheat and corn. In Scotland today, about 700 potato varieties are held in a government reference collection, while in Peru, every genetic aspect of the potato is being investigated through the Centro Internacional de la Papa. Australia has a potato research station, and in Germany a special institute has listed 3,000 varieties of potatoes in existence today. Yet, while thousands and thousands of potato varieties are grown throughout the world, it seems only a small number of those varieties are produced with any regularity.

New varieties of potatoes are created each year, but not all go on to achieve stardom, notoriety or even popularity. Much has to be taken into consideration before new varieties can even be introduced: their resistance to disease and viruses, their suitability for various uses and their yield and storage capabilities, for instance.

What's in a Name?

In Canada we use the name Elizabeth; in Ireland the name is Ilish. Potatoes are much the same. For instance, in the U.K. we have King Edwards for baking, the red-skinned Desiree for roast spuds, the prettily named Maris Piper for chips or fries and the yellow-fleshed Wilja or Nicola for boiling. In Canada we choose Russet Burbank or Russet Norkotah for roasting, baking or mashing, Yukon Golds for boiling or roasting (and really just about anything) and round reds like Chieftain or Rideau for salads and gratins.

The classifications of potatoes—the distinctions that relate to their use—are probably of more use to the average home cook than the variety names. Having said that, it is quite true that you can use any potato for any culinary use. *You will get the best results and the most eating satisfaction, however, when you choose the right type for the task.*

The Right Type for the Task

Simply put, potatoes are really of two distinct types—floury or waxy. Floury potatoes are mealier because they are higher in starch and lower in water than the other type. They make terrific bakers, mashers, roasters, chips or fries. Floury potatoes tend to break up when cooked, which is why they make great mashed potatoes but are a poor candidate for, say, the classic North American–style potato salad in which we like the potato pieces to remain intact. Waxy potatoes are firmer fleshed, higher in water and lower in starch than floury potatoes. Waxy potatoes hold their shape when cooked, so they are best for salads, gratins, boiling, steaming or sautéing.

"All-purpose" potatoes, those that have a relatively even balance of water and starch and are meant to be good for everything, are sort of a one-size-fits-all spud. Think Yukon Gold, everybody's favourite all-rounder.

Have you ever wondered what was meant by "old" and "new" potatoes? These tags refer to the stages of potato growth: regardless of the variety, new potatoes are the current season's crop while old potatoes are those that have been stored from last year's crop.

"Early," "second early" and "main crop" are terms used to describe how long it will take for a particular potato variety to mature fully, generally 70 days for early varieties, 90 days for second early varieties and 120 to 140 days for main crop varieties. Of course, any potato can be harvested before its maturity date and will simply have different characteristics than if it were mature.

No matter where you live in the world, early refers to new potatoes that are available from the current crop. Second early potatoes are still thought of as new potatoes but will have skin that is slightly more mature. Finally, main crop potatoes are available toward the end of the current growing season. These potatoes are stored through the winter and on hand in markets until the next season begins. Just to complicate things, in today's global supermarkets not all early potatoes are waxy and not all late potatoes are floury because some potatoes are picked young when they are still small, as well as at their mature size, and because we import new potatoes from other places when locally grown new potatoes are not available.

The good news is that many large supermarket chains nowadays provide information about the type of potato, its uses and its characteristics right in the produce section alongside the bins of potatoes.

Growing Your Own

If you have even a little bit of garden in which to grow vegetables, you owe it to yourself to plant a few seed potatoes for the sheer thrill of it.

Potatoes are, I think, ridiculously easy to grow. If space is at a premium, consider growing early potato varieties as they require less room. They will grow quickly but generally have a lower yield than varieties that mature more slowly. This past summer, from a planting of about 2 pounds (1 kg) of seed potatoes I grew close to 50 pounds (23 kg) of spuds—so be ready!

Potatoes are adaptable and can do well in either light or heavy soils, but they do require good drainage in a relatively open site and about 20 inches (51 cm) of rainfall or irrigation throughout the season. As a classic cool season crop, potatoes grow best at 61°F to 64°F (16°C–18°C) and require (depending on the variety) a growing season of 70 to 140 frost-free days.

Make sure to choose a potato variety that is recommended for your area. Use seed potatoes that are certified to be disease free, that is, harvested from crops that are free of viruses. Cut seed potatoes into chunks; each chunk should have at least two "eyes," from which the sprouts will emerge. Let the cut surfaces dry over before planting. Plant when the sprouts are about 3/4-inch (2 cm) long and when the risk of frost is gone. Mound up the planting furrows to a depth of about 6 inches (15 cm), and space the tubers 23 inches to 27 inches (60–70 cm) apart (half this distance for early varieties). Cultivate between the rows to nip weeds in the bud, mounding the soil as you do so. As potatoes form close to the surface, mounding the soil is doubly important as it prevents them from greening due to exposure to light.

Harvesting will depend on the variety of potato. For early varieties, start digging the egg-sized potatoes as the flowers open. New potatoes can be dug when the lower leaves of the plant turn yellow, usually about three weeks after flowering. Early potatoes will be ready from early to midsummer, second early varieties from late summer to early autumn and main crop potatoes from early to mid-autumn. Leave healthy main crop potatoes in the ground for as long as possible. As early autumn approaches, cut back the stems (called the haulm) of each plant to about two inches (5 cm) above ground level. Leave the potatoes in the ground for another two weeks (be slug wary) to allow their skins to mature and harden before harvesting.

Selecting and Storing

When buying potatoes, look for firm, dry, smooth unblemished potatoes that are free of sprouts or green areas. Green patches on potatoes can be attributed to their being exposed to light, resulting in the formation of a toxic alkaloid called solanine. Eaten in any quantity, green potatoes will cause stomach upset and worse, so avoid them at all costs. One or two areas of green can be cut away, but potatoes with extensive areas of green should be discarded.

If you are planning to store your own homegrown potatoes, harvest them on a dry, sunny day and allow them to lie in the sun for a couple of hours before storing. Don't wash away the dirt clinging to the potatoes before storing them; it helps to retain their freshness and keeps them in better shape. Don't store potatoes with or near onions because a gas released by onions can cause potatoes to spoil. Store unwashed potatoes in a dry, dark, cool place—not in the refrigerator.

New potatoes, however, with their thin skins, don't keep as well as other varieties, so buy or harvest them when needed and store them in the refrigerator.

Fancy-schmancy—sometimes all you really want is the straight spuds, and that's what this batch of simple potato preparations is all about. Here is the quick, definitive guide to roasting, mashing, baking and frying potatoes, with a few basic variations on those themes thrown in. Simple? Sure, but unfailingly stupendous.

the classic potato

Roasties

Now, the whole thing about roast spuds—or roasties—is the to-parboil-or-not-to-parboil debate. When I'm feeling a little lazy and impatient, I favour the latter, preferring to just roast the raw spuds tossed with a little good olive oil or, if I am roasting beef or pork, setting the potatoes round it to crisp up with the fat from the meat. However, I must admit that pre-cooking them for 10 minutes or so before roasting does seem to result in crisper roasties. Peeling gives you a crustier exterior, but leaving the skins intact is quicker and a little more nutritious—try both methods and see which you prefer. If you do parboil, rough up the edges of the spuds a bit with the tines of a fork before adding to the pan as doing so will make the roasties even crispier.

6 large floury potatoes, peeled, cut into uniform chunks
Salt

1/4 cup (60 mL) olive oil or preferred fat
Salt and freshly ground pepper

If parboiling, place the potatoes in a large saucepan and just cover them with cold water. Add a good pinch of salt, bring to a boil, reduce the heat and simmer the potatoes for 10 to 12 minutes. Drain them well and shake the pot back and forth over very low heat to dry the potatoes completely.

Preheat the oven to 400°F (200°C). Toss the potatoes in the oil in a roasting pan large enough to accommodate them in one layer. Roast the potatoes for about 40 to 45 minutes, turning them once or twice to encourage even roasting. Season with salt and pepper and serve.

Garlic Roasties with Rosemary

MAKES 4 TO 6 SERVINGS

6 large floury potatoes, scrubbed, cut into
   uniform chunks

12 cloves garlic, unpeeled

1/4 cup (60 mL) olive oil

2 tsp (10 mL) dried rosemary

Salt and freshly ground pepper

Preheat the oven to 400°F (200°C). Toss all the ingredients together in a roasting pan large enough to accommodate the potatoes in one layer. Roast the potatoes for about 1 hour, turning them once or twice to encourage even roasting.

 If you plan to grow your own potatoes, remember that the plants take up quite a bit of space, so it's a good idea to grow them in a separate patch. If you grow them with other plants, corn, lettuce, radishes, eggplant and cabbage all make good neighbours for potatoes. Nearby, grow some catnip, coriander, horseradish or onions, as they will deter the dreaded potato beetle. Potatoes won't do well next to apples, pumpkin, squash, raspberries, tomatoes, cucumbers or sunflowers. Beans are a doubly good choice to plant alongside potatoes because the plants protect each other from pests.

I have made these standby spuds more times than I can count. They are simple to put together and very good with roast pork or lamb. I don't peel the garlic because everyone has fun squishing the sweet, nutty cloves out of their skins and eating the soft garlic along with the spuds.

No-Hassle Hasselbacks

Hasselbacks are curious-looking Swedish-style roasties that are made by keeping the potato whole, thinly slicing it crosswise part of the way through and adding a little oil before roasting. As it cooks, the potato opens up like a little edible fan to become beautifully crispy. Sometimes, fresh bay leaves are inserted between the slices. I like to add a little grated Parmesan and a smidge of butter to each potato just to gild the lily a bit.

MAKES 4 TO 6 SERVINGS

6 large floury potatoes, peeled
3 tbsp (45 mL) olive oil
2 tbsp (30 mL) butter, melted

Salt and freshly ground pepper
1/3 cup (75 mL) grated Parmesan cheese

Preheat the oven to 375°F (190°C). Keep the potatoes in a bowl of cold water as you work. Using a sharp knife, thinly slice a bit off one side of each potato to make a base. Place the potato, base down, on a large spoon. (The spoon will act as a guide to keep you from cutting right through the potato.) Make incisions across the potato, about 1/8-inch (3 mm) apart. Now, combine the olive oil with the butter. Place the potatoes in an ovenproof dish and pour the oil and butter mixture over the potatoes, seasoning them with salt and pepper and tossing them so that they are well coated. Roast the potatoes for about 50 minutes. Sprinkle the cheese over the potatoes, toss them to coat with the cheese and bake another 10 minutes, or until the potatoes are crusty and golden brown.

Potatoes love the dark. Unless you have a cool, dark, dry root cellar or similar storage facility, buy just a few pounds of potatoes at a time, rather than vast quantities. Never store potatoes in a plastic bag. Keep them in a brown paper bag or a vegetable bin in a cool, dark, dry place.

Exotic Spiced Roasties

FOR THE SPICE MIXTURE:
  (makes about 1/2 cup/125 mL)

1 tbsp (15 mL) cardamom

1 tbsp (15 mL) cayenne pepper

1 tbsp (15 mL) coriander

1 tbsp (15 mL) cumin

1 tbsp (15 mL) paprika

1 tsp (5 mL) cinnamon

1 tsp (5 mL) cloves

1 tsp (5 mL) freshly ground pepper

1 tsp (5 mL) nutmeg

1 tsp (5 mL) salt

1 tsp (5 mL) sugar

1 tsp (5 mL) turmeric

FOR THE POTATOES:

2 tbsp (30 mL) olive oil

1 lb (500 g) new potatoes, scrubbed

Preheat the oven to 400°F (200°C). In a small mixing bowl, combine all the ingredients for the spice mixture and mix together well. Store in a tightly sealed container.

Brush a little of the olive oil over a baking sheet. Prick the potatoes a couple of times each with a fork. Put all the potatoes in a good-sized mixing bowl, add the remaining oil and 1 to 2 tablespoons (15–30 mL) of the spice mixture. Toss the potatoes until they are well coated with the spices. Place the potatoes on the baking sheet and roast them for 45 minutes to 1 hour, turning them once or twice. Serve immediately.

Use new potatoes for this preparation and keep them whole. The spice combo in this recipe lends an Indian influence to food and can be used as a dry rub on boneless chicken or pork chops before grilling or searing. You will have more of the spice mixture than you need for this recipe, but it is a great pantry staple and, once you have tasted these potatoes, you'll make them often. Try serving them as an appetizer, presented on the end of a wooden skewer, with a cooling accompaniment of plain yogurt combined with fresh chopped mint and coriander.

Classic Mash de Luxe

There are those who maintain you can make mashed potatoes with waxy potatoes. I think that is heresy and the surest way to get lumpy mash, which in this cook's opinion is nothing to be proud of. I should also point out here that while many cooks swear by potato ricers, food mills, hand-held blenders and the like, I have never used anything but my old standard potato masher and a couple of steps learned at my Mum's elbow (see instructions). You can easily cut back on the fat content of this recipe by omitting all but a little butter and using buttermilk in place of cream or whole milk. Use Yukon Golds if you choose the reduced-fat method because they already taste buttery and make great mash (as does, by the way, any good, fresh main crop potato).

MAKES 4 TO 6 SERVINGS

2 lbs (1 kg) floury potatoes, peeled, quartered

1 tsp (5 mL) salt

1/2 cup (125 mL) butter

1/2 cup (125 mL) heavy cream

3/4 cup (150 mL) whole milk (approx.)

Choose a medium-sized saucepan; if the pot is too big, you are likely to use too much water and that will result in, horrors, watery mash. Add the potatoes to the saucepan and just cover with cold water. Stir in the salt. Taste the water at this point; you should be able to taste the salt slightly; if you can't, add a little more—remember, mashed potatoes are nothing without the right amount of salt. Adding it after they are cooked just doesn't work. Cover the saucepan loosely and place it on high heat. When the water has come to a boil, reduce the heat to medium, put the lid completely on the saucepan and boil the potatoes gently for about 20 minutes. Test one of the potatoes with the tip of a paring knife. When the potatoes are tender all the way through, remove them from the heat and drain, keeping them in the saucepan. (Use the potato water in soups or, if you are roasting meat at the same time, to make terrific gravy.) Return the saucepan to the heat, turning it down as low as possible or off entirely so that you're just using the residual heat in the element. Shake the saucepan on the element a few times, until all traces of moisture have evaporated from the potatoes. This step is really important to the success of your mash.

Now then, with the saucepan still on the element, add the butter in one go and mash it well into the potatoes. Gradually add the cream and milk, mashing well after each addition; the pot should still be on the element, keeping the potatoes hot. Once all the cream and milk have been added, bang the masher on the side of the saucepan to get any remaining potato back into the pot. Tilt the saucepan slightly and, using a flat whisk, wooden spoon or a good-sized fork, very quickly stir the potatoes round and round, incorporating a little air into the mash. At this point you may decide that your mixture needs a little more butter, cream or milk; if so, add it and continue stirring. When you have achieved a nice, smooth, creamy yet fluffy mass, use a clean tea towel or napkin to cover the surface of the mashed potatoes and replace the saucepan lid. The cloth will absorb any moisture and keep the mash hot. Serve with a modicum of butter and a proud smile.

 A Scottish immigrant from the Isle of Skye, Lord Selkirk, settled in an area known as Orwell Point on P.E.I. He brought potatoes with him from Scotland, and for many years the new Canadian community in which he lived thrived on them, along with locally caught cod.

Variations on
the theme of Mash

All of these distinct preparations are variations on the basic mashed potato recipe.

Garlic Mash

You can either blanch unpeeled garlic cloves in a little boiling water for a couple of minutes before squeezing the cloves into the mashed potatoes, or roast the garlic in the oven until soft. Easiest of all, peel the garlic cloves and add them to the potatoes toward the end of the cooking time. After draining, just mash the garlic along with the spuds. On average, use a whole head of garlic, separated into cloves, per pound (500 g) of potato.

Big Cheese Mash

Choose a strong-flavoured cheese like old white Cheddar, Gruyère, fontina or Parmigiano-Reggiano. Start with about 1/2 cup (125 mL) grated or shredded cheese, adding a little more if you want a more pronounced taste. Gorgonzola is a nice addition if you are planning to serve the potatoes alongside a hefty steak. Alternatively, add the cheese to the mashed potatoes along with some sautéed onion, a couple of egg yolks and a little paprika, place the mixture in a lightly greased pan and bake until golden brown.

Med Mash

Forget the butter and cream and instead whisk a really good extra virgin olive oil into your mash. Add a handful of finely chopped fresh herbs, perhaps a mixture of basil and parsley, and even a few finely chopped bits of sun-dried tomato and Parmigiano-Reggiano.

Roots Mash

Cook and mash separately an amount of carrots, celeriac, Jerusalem artichokes, turnips, parsnips or any root vegetable you like (even beets!) equal to the amount of potatoes, and swirl the two mashes together for a lovely contrast in colour and flavour.

New Crushed Potatoes

My Mum used to cover halves of new potatoes with boiling water, cook them till tender, drain them and then crush them slightly against the sides of the pot, sometimes with a little chopped parsley and butter. I've had this same "lazy mash" in more than one contemporary restaurant, as chefs have discovered that its pleasing texture goes well beneath pieces of grilled fish or beef. You can vary the basic recipe with olive oil and bits of finely chopped mint, green onion or other fresh herbs.

 While it has long been maintained that Sir Walter Raleigh brought the potato to Ireland in the 1590s, there is no actual evidence to support this theory. According to the commonly accepted story, he gave handfuls of the tubers to his gardeners at the property he owned in Cork, who planted them without comprehending what they were exactly.

The Only Baked Potato

Whose idea was it originally to wrap a perfectly good potato in foil before placing it in the oven to bake? Besides being a colossal waste of time and foil, that silliness results in a steamed potato, never, ever baked. A great baked potato is a gift from heaven. The best, freshest ones remain in your mind for years afterward, forcing you to repeat the experience as often as possible. Remember the huge baked Idaho potatoes they served at the tony Four Seasons Restaurant in NYC? Back in the 1980s, the restaurant used to offer a $9 "Power Lunch"—a perfectly baked potato, split, drenched in extra virgin olive oil and adorned with truffles.

Large baking potatoes
Olive oil (optional)
Coarse salt (optional)

All you need do to achieve baked potato perfection is choose big, sound baking potatoes of uniform size, scrub them clean and stick them in a preheated 400°F (200°C) oven for a little over an hour. They will be cooked through in an hour, but leaving them in the oven a wee bit longer results in those baked potatoes with a crackly good exterior and a fluffy, creamy interior. If you like, cut a shallow X into the top of each potato so that you can do that fancy thing that steakhouse chefs do to make the potato open up budlike, ready to receive a few chunks of butter. Some people like to rub potatoes with olive oil and coarse salt before baking them—can't hurt. And, if you're in a hurry, halve the potato lengthwise, brush each cut side with olive oil and bake. Half—baked!

(For more great baked potato ideas, see page 44.)

The Virtuous Chip

MAKES 4 TO 6 SERVINGS

6 large floury potatoes, peeled or not
2–3 tbsp (30–45 mL) vegetable oil
Salt and freshly ground pepper

Preheat the oven to 400°F (200°C). Slice the potatoes into thick chips. Toss them with the oil, salt and pepper and transfer them to a baking sheet. Bake the potatoes for about 45 minutes until golden brown and cooked through, turning them once or twice to encourage even browning.

For those who eschew fat in all its wondrous forms, I offer this recipe for chips that are almost as good as the real thing. Try varying this oven-chip recipe by sprinkling a little curry or chili powder over the potatoes along with the oil.

Chips, fries, frites, sautés, home fries and hash browns. It seems to me that potatoes and fat were made for each other, whether in the form of chunky English chips, delicate Belgian frites with mayo or good old home fries.

English Chips

MAKES 4 TO 6 SERVINGS

6 large floury potatoes
Vegetable oil

These are the chips that have sustained a nation—the U.K.—especially those late-night pub-crawlers searching for something of real substance to soak up gallons of ale. (This country is so enamoured of the fried potato that it holds a National Chip Week each year—hurrah!) While there's nothing quite like standing on a damp corner and eating them straight out of the chip shop paper, these chips are also wonderful piled high on a plate, doused with malt vinegar and sprinkled with salt. The reason those chip shop chips taste so wonderful is because they are fried twice—the first time for about 6 minutes or so, then again in hotter oil for a couple of minutes. Use a deep-fryer and a frying basket; otherwise improvise with a good-sized, heavy-based deep pot. Use enough oil to fill it halfway.

Peel the potatoes and slice them into nice, thick pieces—you're not making frites here, so I suggest lengthwise slices about 2-inches (5 cm) long and at least 1/2-inch (1 cm) wide. (Thick-cut chips absorb less oil than thin ones, by the way.) Now, as you slice, plop the potatoes into a bowl of cold water. Once you have cut all the potatoes, leave them in the water for at least 15 minutes, longer if you have the time. Heat the oil to 350°F (180°C). If you are not using a deep-fryer, which has a built-in gauge, use a candy thermometer to gauge the temperature of the oil. Drain the chips and dry them thoroughly on paper toweling or a clean tea towel. They must be absolutely dry. Carefully add the potatoes, in batches, to the hot oil and fry until they are just beginning to colour and are soft. Lift the chips from the fat and drain them on paper toweling. They can sit at this point for some time, or at least for 10 minutes, before the second fry. Now, increase the heat so that the oil reaches 400°F (200°C). Return the chips to the oil and cook for the second time, again in batches, until the chips are crisp and golden, about 3 to 5 minutes. Drain again and serve at once.

Frites à la Kingsmill

MAKES 6 TO 8 SERVINGS

8 large russet potatoes, peeled
Vegetable oil
Salt

Cut the potatoes into 1/4-inch (5 mm) square fries the length of the potato. Fill a 3-quart (3 L) pot one-third full of vegetable oil. Using a candy thermometer to gauge the temperature, heat the oil to 375°F (190°C). Add a third of the frites to the oil. Watch the thermometer closely. When the temperature drops to 300°F (150°C), immediately remove the fries to a baking sheet and let cool. Repeat the process for the remaining potatoes.

For the second fry, just before serving heat the oil to 385°F (195°C); add a quarter of the partially cooked fries. (If the temperature drops too quickly, cook fewer fries in the next batch.) Stir the fries around to crisp them. When they are golden brown, in about 3 minutes, remove them to a baking sheet or bowl and sprinkle them generously with salt. Repeat until all the fries are done. If the first batch is too cool by the end of the process, drop the cool fries back into the hot oil for a few seconds to revive them. Serve at once. (Make a batch of the wonderfully easy aïoli on page 110 as a classic accompaniment to these great frites.)

Reprinted with permission of Key Porter Books from Home Bistro *by David Kingsmill. © David Kingsmill, 1996.*

Potatoes fried in fat, deep or otherwise, speak to the hedonist in all of us. My good friend David Kingsmill, fellow food hound and the very definition of bon vivant, said in his terrific book Home Bistro *(Key Porter Books, 1996) that real frites are "caramel-coloured and crisp on the outside ... tender on the inside ... when they come to the table all salted and hot, they go craack!" Kingsmill maintains that the difference between making great chips and great frites is all a matter of movement: chips should sit still in hot fat while great frites need to be agitated. And don't use a deep-fryer because frites need "a fluctuating oil temperature," not a constant one. Now that I have given my buddy a shameless plug, I don't think he'll mind if I use his recipe.*

Roadhouse Hash Browns

MAKES 4 TO 6 SERVINGS

If you want to really thrill someone at breakfast, get up first and make these classic hash brown potatoes that require only the gift of time to make them great. The night before, make extra potatoes for dinner so that you will have ready leftovers. You can vary these hash browns as you like with bits of cooked ham, bacon or crumbled corned beef. Just before they are ready, try breaking three or four eggs into the centre of the potatoes, cover and cook until the tops of the eggs are slightly set. Serve at once.

1/4 cup (60 mL) olive oil
1 tbsp (15 mL) butter
1 onion, finely chopped

6 medium leftover boiled potatoes, diced
Salt and freshly ground pepper

Heat the olive oil and the butter in a good-sized skillet, preferably a cast-iron skillet, and sauté the onion until softened. Add the potatoes and salt and pepper. Using a spatula, spread the potatoes evenly over the surface of the pan, pressing them down as they cook for about 20 minutes, or until golden brown on the bottom. Place a plate over the skillet, flip it over and return the hash browns to the skillet, uncooked side down. Continue to cook, pressing down as before, until the hash browns are golden brown and crispy.

O'Brien Home Fries

MAKES 4 TO 6 SERVINGS

1/4 cup (60 mL) olive oil

1 tbsp (15 mL) butter

1 green bell pepper, chopped

1 onion, sliced

6 medium leftover boiled potatoes, diced

1 tsp (5 mL) cayenne pepper

Salt and freshly ground pepper

3/4 cup (150 mL) grated Cheddar, Asiago or
    other strong-flavoured cheese

Combine the olive oil and the butter in a good-sized skillet and sauté the bell pepper and onion for a few minutes until softened. Add the potatoes and seasonings and stir to combine well. Continue to cook for about 15 to 20 minutes, stirring occasionally so as to crisp up the potatoes. A few minutes before they are finished, stir the cheese into the mixture. Serve immediately.

Well, I don't know who O'Brien was, but I've always liked his or her home fries that feature onion, nubs of green bell pepper and a bit of grated cheese. Great with hefty sausages, smoked fish or eggs.

The *vitelotte* is an unusual black-skinned tuber with purplish blue flesh that has a waxy, firm texture and slightly nutty flavour. It is also known as the *truffe de Chine*—Chinese truffle—or truffle potato because of its resemblance to the expensive fungus. The unique flesh colour doesn't fade when this tuber is cooked, making it a favourite of chefs looking to provide the unusual on their menus.

Soufflé Potatoes

MAKES 4 SERVINGS

We have the French to thank for these exquisite spuds. Apparently, this wonderful dish was created in the 17th century when Louis XIV's chef tried to salvage some limp pommes frites that he had made as part of a detailed dinner. The king and his entourage arrived late, the frites were cold and soggy and the chef was horrified. In a mad attempt to revive them, he put the cold potatoes in very hot fat. They puffed up and, voilà, he'd created a glorious new way to enjoy potatoes. Even though this recipe will serve four, make these only for yourself and someone you love truly, madly, deeply. Politically incorrect as it may be, if you have a large quantity of clarified beef fat in your refrigerator, now's the time to use it.

4 large floury potatoes, peeled
Vegetable oil for deep-frying
Salt

Slice the potatoes lengthwise into even slices about 1/4-inch (5 mm) thick. Soak the slices in ice water for 20 minutes. Heat the oil to 300°F (150°C) in a deep-fryer or other heavy-based pot. (The accuracy of the oil temperature is vital, so if you are not using a deep-fryer with a gauge, use a candy thermometer to gauge the temperature of the oil.) Drain the potatoes and pat dry. Cook a few slices of potato at a time, turning them once, until nearly soft, which should take a few minutes; you don't want them to brown. Remove the potatoes from the fat and transfer them to paper toweling. Allow them to cool to room temperature.

When you are ready to cook them a second time, increase the heat of the oil to 400°F (200°C). Return a few of the potato slices to the hot fat. Now, cook them until they are puffy and golden brown, transferring them gently to more paper toweling as you work. Continue until all the slices are cooked. Ideally, they should be eaten straight away, as they will deflate quickly. If they do, you can always return them to the hot fat for a few seconds. Sprinkle with a little salt and serve.

Classic Scalloped Spuds

MAKES 4 TO 6 SERVINGS

6 tbsp (90 mL) butter

6 large potatoes, peeled, thinly sliced

1 large white onion, thinly sliced

1/4 cup (60 mL) all-purpose flour (approx.)

Salt and freshly ground pepper

1 cup (250 mL) whole milk

1 cup (250 mL) table cream (or heavy cream)

Preheat the oven to 325°F (160°C). Use a little of the butter to lightly grease a 10-inch (25 cm) oval gratin dish. What you want is four layers of potatoes and onion, sprinkled lightly with flour, dotted with butter and lightly seasoned. Start with a layer of potato. Scatter on some onion, flour, butter and salt and pepper. Repeat the process, ending with potatoes and the last bit of butter. Lightly season the surface with salt and pepper and transfer the gratin dish to a baking sheet covered with parchment paper or foil. In a bowl, combine the milk and cream. Place the baking tray holding the gratin on the middle rack of the oven. Carefully pour the milk mixture evenly over the potatoes, making sure you just cover the potatoes (don't overfill). Loosely cover the dish with foil (it should not touch the surface of the potatoes) and bake for 1 hour. Remove the foil, increase the oven temperature to 375°F (190°C) and continue to bake until the scalloped potatoes are golden brown and bubbly.

I grew up with scalloped potatoes— not potatoes au gratin. These days, I seem to make sophisticated gratins more than old-fashioned scalloped potatoes, gratins made with expensive cheese and no onion. But there is something decidedly comforting about real scalloped potatoes, cooked at a lower heat for a longer period of time, served with a clove-studded ham and buttered green cabbage. Floury potatoes will produce scalloped potatoes that come together in a mass, whereas using waxy potatoes, or all-purpose spuds (like Yukon Golds), will give you a more layered version. Either way, scalloped spuds are great.

Classic Potato Gratin

There is no end of variations on this theme. You can (as I have done here) add that expensive cheese (Gruyère is best for this, I think) or chopped fresh herbs or green onion. If you add sliced, sautéed onions to this basic recipe, you will create what the French call boulangère *potatoes, and very good they are. Play around with this recipe as you like—you won't be marked later on your creation.*

MAKES 4 TO 6 SERVINGS

3 tbsp (45 mL) butter
6 large potatoes, peeled, thinly sliced
2 cloves garlic, chopped
Salt and freshly ground pepper
3/4 cup (150 mL) grated Gruyère cheese

1/2 cup (125 mL) grated Parmesan cheese
2 cups (500 mL) chicken stock
1/4 cup (50 mL) chopped fresh flat-leaf parsley

Preheat the oven to 350°F (180°C). Use a little of the butter to lightly grease a 10-inch (25 cm) oval gratin dish. Arrange a third of the sliced potatoes with a little of the garlic, salt and pepper in the gratin dish. Repeat with the remaining potatoes and garlic, seasoning as you work. Use your hands to press the potatoes down into the dish. Lightly season the surface and dot with the remaining butter. In a bowl, mix the two cheeses together well. Transfer the gratin dish to a baking sheet covered with parchment paper or foil. Place the baking sheet holding the gratin dish on the middle rack of the oven. Carefully pour the chicken stock evenly over the potatoes, making sure you just cover the potatoes (don't over-fill). Cover the surface evenly with the cheese mixture. Bake for 1 hour and 15 minutes, or until the potatoes are cooked through and the top of the gratin is golden brown and bubbly. (If the top browns too quickly, cover the gratin loosely with foil for the last bit of cooking time.) Remove the gratin from the oven and let sit for 5 minutes or so before serving sprinkled with parsley.

Old-fashioned Creamed Potatoes

MAKES 4 SERVINGS

16 small new potatoes, scrubbed, left whole

1 tsp (5 mL) salt

2 tbsp (30 mL) butter

2 tbsp (30 mL) all-purpose flour

1 cup (250 mL) table cream

1/4 cup (60 mL) chopped fresh chives

Put the potatoes in a large saucepan. Cover with boiling water, add the salt, stir, cover loosely and boil gently until the potatoes are tender, about 20 minutes or so. Drain, but retain a little bit of cooking water. Add the butter to the potatoes and gently toss them to coat. Add the flour and gently toss until the buttered potatoes have taken up all the flour. Place the pan on low heat and add the cream, stirring the potatoes gently. Cook gently until the sauce thickens, adding a little more cream, milk or reserved cooking water if the mixture becomes too thick. Transfer the potatoes to a warmed serving bowl and sprinkle with chives before serving.

Not many people make these anymore—or for that matter, any vegetables in a cream sauce—but you should try this recipe, at least once, when tiny new spuds are plentiful. Let the cooked potatoes cool before attempting to peel them. This dish is lovely with roast chicken or pork.

 Not surprisingly, the Irish had a number of rituals associated with potatoes. In Cork, the first potatoes were always unearthed on June 29. In Galway, it was forbidden to dig potatoes until the last Sunday in July. Residents of County Mayo celebrated the close of the harvest with a feast, and in Tipperary the arrival of new potatoes on the table was met with "May we all be alive and happy this time 12 months."

Packed with flavour appeal, these recipes really showcase just how incredibly useful, versatile and delicious the potato can be. All of the following recipes can be used as appetizers, midnight snacks, brunch items, mini-meals or as first courses for stylish sit-down suppers. There are soups to nourish and impress, hors d'oeuvres for an elegant cocktail gathering or hearty fare for a group of foot-ball fanatics—potatoes for couch potatoes!

the appetizing potato

Baked Baby Reds with Crème Fraîche & Caviar

MAKES 30 HORS D'OEUVRES

Watch the faces of your guests when you bring these lovely little spuds into the room. Here we have one perfect potato bite made even more special with a little crown of crème fraîche and a bit of caviar—I'll leave the type to you and your budget. If you like, use bits of smoked salmon, tiny shrimp or crisp bacon in place of the caviar, or blend a small piece of strong blue cheese with a little of the crème fraîche and use it to top these sweet little spuds. You will have more than you need of the crème fraîche for this recipe, but it keeps up to 10 days refrigerated. Make it a day ahead.

FOR THE CRÈME FRAÎCHE:
1 cup (250 mL) heavy cream
2 tbsp (30 mL) buttermilk or sour cream

FOR THE POTATOES:
30 small new red potatoes, washed
3/4 cup (175 mL) crème fraîche
1/2 oz (15 g) caviar
Sprigs of fresh chervil

To make the crème fraîche, gently warm the heavy cream. Remove it from the heat and combine it with the buttermilk or sour cream in a glass bowl. Mix well, cover and let stand at room temperature overnight. Give the mixture a good stir once it has thickened, then cover and refrigerate. It will thicken even more once chilled.

Preheat the oven to 375°F (190°C). Using a sharp knife, very thinly slice a bit off one end of each potato to form a base. Place the potatoes on a baking sheet and bake until tender, about 45 minutes. Let cool slightly. Make a small X in the top of each potato and push the sides of the potato toward each other. Top each potato with a bit of crème fraîche, a smidge of caviar and a chervil leaf. Serve immediately.

Potato & Two Leek Soup

MAKES 4 TO 6 SERVINGS

2 tbsp (30 mL) butter

1 tbsp (15 mL) olive oil

3 large leeks, trimmed, washed, thinly sliced

1 clove garlic, minced

1 white onion, finely chopped

3 large floury potatoes, peeled, diced

4 cups (1 L) chicken broth or full-flavoured vegetable broth

1 cup (250 mL) heavy cream

Salt and freshly ground pepper

Sautéed leeks or lengths of fresh chives

In a large saucepan, melt the butter and oil over medium heat. Add the leeks, garlic and onion and sauté, stirring occasionally, until the vegetables are softened, about 5 minutes. Do not allow the vegetables to brown. Add the potatoes and broth, bring to a boil, reduce the heat, cover and let simmer for about 25 minutes, stirring now and then. When the potatoes are quite soft, use a hand-held blender to purée the soup (or purée it in small batches in a food processor or blender) until relatively smooth. Wipe the saucepan clean, return the soup to the pan and add the cream and salt and pepper. If the soup is thicker than you would like, add a little milk and simmer the soup until heated through. Serve hot garnished with sautéed leeks or fresh chives.

Here is a classic soup that, if served chilled, becomes even more sophisticated (and it gets a new name, too: vichyssoise). I prefer it as a winter warmer and like to serve it with a sprinkle of sautéed leeks. Deep-frying strands of leeks will make them frizzled and produce a nice chef-style garnish. Make sure to wash the leeks thoroughly by slitting them open lengthwise and spreading them apart while rinsing them clean under cold running water.

Potato Focaccia

The definitive, rustic leavened bread, focaccia can be treated to an endless number of toppings, but I think this one, with thin slices of unpeeled, waxy potatoes and fresh rosemary, is really ace. It is as good served at room temperature as it is served warm. You can vary this recipe by piling the finished bread with mounds of silky prosciutto or fresh arugula drizzled with a little extra virgin olive oil ... oh yeah.

MAKES TWO 10-INCH (25 CM) BREADS

FOR THE DOUGH:

Pinch of sugar

1/2 cup (125 mL) lukewarm water

2 1/2 tsp (12 mL) active dry yeast

2 tsp (10 mL) salt

2 tsp (10 mL) sugar

1 cup (250 mL) lukewarm water

5–6 cups (1.25–1.5 L) bread flour or all-purpose flour

Olive oil

FOR THE TOPPING:

1 lb (500 g) red-skinned waxy potatoes, unpeeled

3 sprigs fresh rosemary

4 cloves garlic, minced

1 cup (250 mL) grated Parmesan cheese

1/4 cup (60 mL) extra virgin olive oil

Salt and freshly ground pepper

Olive oil (optional)

Warm a measuring cup with hot tap water; drain. In the warm cup, dissolve a pinch of sugar in the 1/2 cup (125 mL) lukewarm water. Sprinkle the yeast over the surface; let stand for 10 minutes, or until frothy.

In a large mixing bowl, combine the yeast mixture, salt, 2 tsp (10 mL) sugar and 1 cup (250 mL) lukewarm water. Stir in the flour, 1 cup (250 mL) at a time, until a soft dough forms (some flour may remain unused). On a lightly floured surface, knead the dough for 5 minutes, or until it is smooth and elastic, adding enough flour to keep the dough from sticking.

Wipe the bowl clean, lightly coat the surface with a little olive oil and add the dough, turning it to coat it with the oil. Cover the dough with plastic wrap and then a clean tea towel. Let the dough rise in a warm place for 2 hours, or until it has doubled in volume and indentations remain when the dough is poked with two fingers. Punch it down, cover and let rise for about 1 hour while you prepare the topping.

Slice the potatoes very thinly into a large bowl. Strip the leaves from the branches of rosemary, chop the leaves roughly and add them to the potatoes. Add the garlic, cheese and olive oil to the potato mixture and season with salt and pepper. Toss to combine well. Set to one side.

Preheat the oven to 425°F (220°C). Transfer the dough to a lightly floured work surface and divide into two pieces. Pulling and stretching, begin to work the dough into a rectangular shape. Place it on a baking sheet, cover with a clean tea towel and repeat the procedure with the remaining dough. Distribute the potato mixture evenly over the two breads, drizzle with a little more olive oil, if desired, and bake the breads in the centre of the oven for about 20 to 30 minutes, or until the potatoes are cooked through and the crust is golden and crisp.

 In 1793, Louis XVI and Marie Antoinette had potatoes grown in an experiment on 50 acres of fallow land. In what must have been one of the world's most successful—and earliest—marketing ploys, the king commanded armed troops to guard the growing plants. This caused such attention that curious spectators crept into the grounds at night when the guards were lax, and unearthed and stole the potatoes. If the vegetables were good enough to be guarded, they were most definitely good enough to eat. As a result of this event, for a long time potatoes were called "royal oranges" in France.

The Classic Twice-Baked Jacket

In the U.K., jacket potatoes—baked potatoes—are a big lunch favourite. They are sold in pubs, at outdoor market stalls and by vendors who specialize in them and "nought else," as the characters on Coronation Street always say. Many ingredients would work well as the filling—shrimp and coriander, mushrooms and Gruyère, baked beans and bacon. Here's one version to get your motor running. Serve it with just a bit of butter and, if you must, sour cream.

MAKES 4 TO 8 SERVINGS

4 large baking potatoes, scrubbed

Salt

1 medium onion, sliced

4 cloves garlic, peeled

6 slices back bacon, cooked, chopped

3 green onions, finely chopped

1 cup (250 mL) grated old Cheddar cheese

1/2 cup (125 mL) Taleggio cheese, diced

1/3 cup (75 mL) butter

1/4 cup (60 mL) sour cream

2 tsp (10 mL) chili powder

Salt and freshly ground pepper

Preheat the oven to 425°F (220°C). Slice the potatoes in half lengthwise. Using a sharp knife, diamond score the cut side of each potato (this will make it easier to scoop out the flesh once the potatoes are baked). Season with a little salt. Place the potatoes, cut side down, on a nonstick baking sheet. Loosely pile the slices of onion on the baking sheet and add the cloves of garlic. Bake for 1 hour, or until the potatoes are cooked and tender and the onions and garlic are slightly charred. Remove from the oven. Let cool for a few minutes, and then finely chop the onions and garlic and place them in a mixing bowl. Carefully scoop the potato flesh out of the skins and place it in the bowl with the onions and garlic. Try not to tear or break the potato skins. Mash the potato flesh and add the bacon, green onions, cheeses, butter, sour cream, chili powder and salt and pepper. Combine all ingredients well.

Spoon the mixture into the potato skins, pressing firmly to stuff them well. Return the potatoes to the oven and bake them for another 15 minutes, or until they are heated through and the surface is beginning to crisp up. Serve immediately.

Potato & Roast Garlic Soup with Cheese Toasties

MAKES 4 TO 6 SERVINGS

FOR THE SOUP:

2 heads of garlic, whole

7 cups (1.75 L) chicken stock

4 large boiling potatoes, peeled, diced

Salt and freshly ground pepper

FOR THE CHEESE TOASTIES:

1/2 cup (125 mL) extra virgin olive oil

1 baguette, cut diagonally into 1-inch
  (2.5 cm) slices

1 1/2 cups (375 mL) ricotta cheese

1 cup (250 mL) grated Parmigiano-Reggiano

1/4 cup (60 mL) chopped flat-leaf parsley

This wonderfully warming concoction is a perfect supper for a frigid February evening. Don't worry about the amount of garlic; once it is baked, it becomes quite mellow. Easy to put together, this soup is flat-out delicious and quite substantial, especially with the floating cheese toasties.

Preheat the oven to 375°F (190°C). Place the two heads of garlic in a little roasting pan and bake them for about 30 minutes until soft. Bring the stock to a boil in a large saucepan, reduce the heat, add the potatoes and cook for 10 minutes. When the garlic is cool enough to handle, squeeze contents of the cloves into the soup. Season with salt and pepper. Simmer the soup for about 15 minutes.

Increase the oven temperature to 400°F (200°C). In a large skillet, heat the olive oil on medium-high heat. In batches, toast the bread slices in the oil for about 1 minute per side, or until golden brown. Drain them on paper toweling. Divide the ricotta among the toasts, spreading it over the surface. Place the toasts on a baking sheet. Sprinkle the toasts with some of the Parmigiano-Reggiano. Bake for 5 minutes, or until the cheese is golden. Sprinkle the toasts with parsley.

Ladle the soup into bowls and place one cheese toast in the centre of each. Serve the remaining toasts and cheese at the table.

Potato Latkes Stack with Smoked Trout

MAKES 4 SERVINGS

This makes a really lovely first course—light and crisp-edged potato latkes topped with a smoked trout and sour cream combination with a peppery tangle of watercress for a base. As this dish is rather filling, choose a main course that is not too demanding and make sure not to make the latkes too large.

FOR THE SMOKED TROUT:
12 oz (375 g) smoked trout fillets,
    skin removed
1/2 cup (125 mL) dry cottage cheese
1/2 cup (125 mL) sour cream
2 tbsp (30 mL) lemon juice
Pinch of cayenne pepper
Salt and freshly ground pepper

FOR THE WATERCRESS BASE:
2 bunches watercress, rinsed, dried
2 tbsp (30 mL) extra virgin olive oil
1 tbsp (15 mL) balsamic vinegar
1 tsp (5 mL) Dijon mustard
Salt and freshly ground pepper

FOR THE LATKES:
2 large potatoes, peeled
2 shallots, minced
1 extra large egg, beaten
1/4 cup (60 mL) all-purpose flour
Salt and freshly ground pepper
1/4 cup (60 mL) olive oil or vegetable oil

In a food processor, purée the fish fillets. Add the cottage cheese and sour cream; blend until smooth. Add the lemon juice, a pinch of cayenne and season with salt and pepper. Process the mixture until just combined. Cover and chill for about 2 hours until ready to use.

After rinsing and drying the watercress, keep it in a plastic bag, chilled until ready to use. In a small bowl, whisk together the olive oil, balsamic vinegar and mustard. Season with salt and pepper. Set to one side.

Preheat the oven to a warm setting. Coarsely grate the potatoes. Transfer them to a colander and press down on the potatoes to remove as much liquid as possible. Put the grated potato in a mixing bowl and add the shallots, egg, flour and salt and pepper. Stir well to thoroughly blend the ingredients. In a large skillet, warm some of the olive oil over medium heat. When the oil is hot, add the potato mixture a large spoonful at a time, forming a roughly round shape. Don't press down on the pancakes as they cook, as this will make them heavy. Just pat them with the back of a spoon or metal spatula. Turn them once or twice and fry until cooked through, about 3 to 4 minutes per side. As you work, transfer the cooked latkes to a paper towel–lined baking sheet and keep them warm in the oven. You should have 8 latkes.

When the latkes are ready, toss the watercress together with the dressing. Place a mound of watercress on each of 4 plates. Top with a latke and a dollop of the smoked trout mixture, sandwiched with another latke and more of the smoked trout mixture. Serve immediately.

Potato & Pepper Tortilla

MAKES 4 SERVINGS

A Spanish tortilla, like an Italian frittata, works well as brunch, lunch, dinner or hors d'oeuvres. Here, I have added the smokiness of roasted red bell pepper to the standard tortilla de patata. Look in specialty food shops for piquillo peppers packed in jars and imported from Spain, or use regular roasted red bell peppers. If the quantity of olive oil seems considerable, remember that this dish comes from the world's largest producer of olive oil, where it is used lavishly. The oil really is central to the success of this dish, so make an effort to look for Spanish olive oil for it. Serve the tortilla warm or at room temperature.

4 large Yukon Gold potatoes, peeled, thinly sliced
1 onion, finely chopped
3/4 cup (175 mL) extra virgin olive oil
Salt and freshly ground pepper

6 large eggs
Salt
3 piquillo peppers or 1 large roasted red bell pepper, peeled, cut into strips

In a large bowl, combine the potatoes and onion well. In a heavy skillet, heat the oil over medium-high heat. Add the potatoes in layers, seasoning each layer with salt and pepper.

Reduce the heat to medium-low. Cook the potatoes, turning often and being careful not to brown them, for 15 to 20 minutes, or until the potatoes are tender. Remove them to a paper towel–lined plate. Reserve oil. Drain, patting the potatoes with more toweling to absorb excess oil. Allow to cool slightly before proceeding.

In a bowl, lightly beat the eggs with some salt. Add the peppers and stir in the potatoes. Let the mixture sit at room temperature for about 10 minutes.

Pour the oil from the skillet into a bowl. Wipe the skillet clean, return 2 tablespoons (30 mL) of the oil to the skillet and place over medium heat. When the oil is hot, add the egg mixture. Cook, shaking the skillet occasionally, for about 4 minutes, or until the tortilla is brown on the bottom.

Place a large plate upside down over the skillet. Flip the tortilla over onto the plate and slip the tortilla back into the skillet. Cook, pressing down on the tortilla and shaking the skillet, for about 4 minutes. Transfer the tortilla to a plate and serve warm or at room temperature, cut into wedges.

Baked Potato Salad
with Blue Cheese Drizzle

MAKES 4 SERVINGS

FOR THE DRESSING:
1/2 cup (125 mL) crumbled
    Gorgonzola cheese
1/4 cup (60 mL) mayonnaise
1/4 cup (60 mL) sour cream
1/4 cup (60 mL) table cream
2 tsp (10 mL) fresh lemon juice
Salt and freshly ground pepper

FOR THE POTATOES:
4 large baking potatoes, scrubbed
4 cups (1 L) baby spinach
3 green onions, finely chopped

Earlier in the book I have mentioned that when you bake potatoes for a longer time than necessary, the exterior gets extra crispy and the flesh even sweeter. This makes them great candidates for this side dish that my husband Ted loves to serve with pan-seared strip loin steaks.

Preheat the oven to 450°F (230°C). While the oven heats, make the dressing by combining the cheese, mayonnaise, sour cream, table cream and lemon juice in a bowl. Use a large fork to slightly mash the cheese, leaving some chunks of it intact. Season with salt and pepper. Cover the dressing and refrigerate until ready to use.

Bake the potatoes for about 1 hour and 30 minutes, longer if you have time. Arrange the baby spinach on 4 plates. When the potatoes are ready, remove from the oven and let them sit for a minute or two. Slice the potatoes lengthwise into halves and then quarters. Divide the potato pieces among the plates. Drizzle the dressing over the potatoes and spinach (if the dressing has thickened too much, add a little cream to thin it out). Sprinkle with the chopped green onions and serve immediately, with extra dressing if desired.

Mum's Potato Bread

These are the comforting little potato breads I wrote about earlier in the book, made by my Uncle Bob, my Auntie Madge and my dear Mum. Not bread in the strict sense of the word, these potato preparations are a specialty of Northern Ireland and go by many different names in that part of the world. To my family, they were always potato bread, anticipated with great delight and even made in batches for Christmas gift giving. The amounts of butter and flour given here are meant to be guidelines; sometimes you may use a little less of each, and at other times you may need to use more to achieve a nice, unsticky dough that rolls out beautifully. These potato breads are the perfect accompaniment to a traditional Northern Irish breakfast, the Ulster Fry. Put on hold any reservations you have about using butter and salt—slather and sprinkle at will.

MAKES 4 TO 6 SERVINGS

5 cups (1.25 L) mashed potatoes

1 cup + 1 tbsp (250 mL + 15 mL)
 all-purpose flour

1/2 cup (125 mL) chilled butter (approx.)

Salt

Warm the oven. Combine the mashed potatoes with half of the flour and half of the butter, using your hands to blend the ingredients as you would when making pastry. When the dough is still a little sticky, turn it out onto a floured surface and work in the remaining flour (use a little more as needed). Knead the dough lightly a few times, and then roll it out to about a 1/2-inch (1 cm) thickness (Uncle Bob's were thicker!). Cut the dough into pie-shaped wedges. Heat a griddle or cast-iron pan over medium-high heat. Melt a bit of the remaining butter and fry the potato breads in batches, cooking them until golden speckled brown on both sides. Keep the cooked breads warm in the oven as you work. Serve them hot with a wee bit more butter and salt.

Potato Soda Bread

MAKES 2 LOAVES

3 cups (750 mL) bread flour or
   all-purpose flour
1 cup (250 mL) whole wheat flour
1 tbsp (15 mL) baking powder
1 tsp (5 mL) baking soda

1 tsp (5 mL) salt
1/4 cup (60 mL) butter
4 medium floury potatoes, boiled, mashed
1 egg
1 3/4 cups (425 mL) buttermilk

Preheat the oven to 375°F (190°C). In a large mixing bowl, combine the two flours, baking powder, baking soda and salt. Add the butter and cut it into the dry ingredients with a pastry blender or fork until the mixture resembles breadcrumbs. Mix in the mashed potato.

In another bowl, whisk together the egg and buttermilk. Make a well in the centre of the dry ingredients and add the egg mixture all at once. Stir to blend well. Turn the dough out onto a lightly floured surface and knead until smooth, about 2 to 3 minutes, using a little bit more flour as needed.

Divide the dough in half and shape each into a round, flat loaf. Using a sharp knife, cut crosses on the top of each loaf. Bake for 35 to 40 minutes. Serve warm with butter.

My Mum used to make dozens of classic Irish soda bread loaves around St. Patrick's Day. This is her basic recipe—a natural evolution of a classic—made even more Irish to my mind with the addition of mashed potatoes. Make this bread when you have a few leftover boiled potatoes.

Kingsmill's Potato Raft

MAKES 2 SERVINGS

2 large baking potatoes, peeled
Vegetable oil as needed
Salt

From my good buddy David Kingsmill comes this lovely potato creation. His words: "Life is full of mistakes. I was once asked on very short notice to invent a Grey Cup snack, so I thought I would reinvent the potato chip. I figured if I got the rounds of potatoes extremely thin, I wouldn't have to go through all the bother of frying twice. So, using the potato peeler, I started slicing a peeled potato directly into the hot oil. Well, the slices stuck together. Couldn't get them to separate to save my life. So I gave up. The result was an attractive irregularly shaped 'raft' of delicately fried spuds." According to its creator, these rafts look fab next to a huge slab of rare prime rib. Now, you're talking.

Using a candy thermometer to gauge the temperature, heat the oil in a large, heavy pot to 375°F (190°C). Using a potato peeler that produces very thin slices, peel slices of the potato directly into the hot oil, as if you were flipping playing cards into a hat. They'll stick together in a raft as they fry. When the raft reaches a serving portion, flip it over to brown the other side. Remove the raft, salt it immediately and keep warm. Repeat for the second raft. Serve the rafts immediately.

Potato Cakes with Pancetta & Fontina

MAKES 4 SERVINGS

8 slices, thinly sliced pancetta (unsmoked Italian bacon)

4–5 leftover boiled potatoes, peeled

Salt and freshly ground pepper

2 tbsp (30 mL) butter

1–2 tbsp (15–30 mL) olive oil

8 fresh sage leaves

6 oz (185 g) fontina cheese, cut into 8 slices

Fry the pancetta until just cooked and barely crisp; don't overcook. Set it to one side. Grate the potatoes on the side of a coarse grater into a shallow dish. Season with salt and pepper, and then shape the grated potato into 8 flattish patties. Melt the butter with the olive oil in a large skillet over medium-high heat. When the butter froths, slide in 4 of the potato cakes using a metal spatula. (If your skillet is not large enough, cook the potato cakes in batches, keeping the cakes warm in a low oven as you work.) Cook the potato cakes for 3 to 4 minutes, or until golden brown and heated through. When all the potato cakes have been cooked, return as many as will fit in one layer to the skillet (you may need a little more oil and butter). Place a piece of pancetta on each potato cake, followed by a leaf of sage and finally a slice of fontina. Cover the skillet with a lid and cook for another minute or two, just until the cheese has melted. Serve immediately.

Here is a great savoury snack that, though quite simple, provides much eating satisfaction. Different from latkes, these crispy potato cakes are made from leftover boiled potatoes and are the perfect vehicle for good quality ham and warm, melting fontina. Yummers. Really nice with a bit of dark, fruity chutney.

Potato & Tomato Cheese Bake

MAKES 4 TO 6 SERVINGS

Great for vegetarians (who eat cheese), this dish makes a lovely main course when served with a bright green broccoli salad. Vary the cheese as you like. It's not really necessary, but if you have time, use a vegetable peeler to remove the skins from the tomatoes.

1/4 cup (60 mL) extra virgin olive oil

6 large Yukon Gold potatoes, scrubbed, cut crosswise into thin slices

3 cloves garlic, minced

2 white onions, thinly sliced

1 lb (500 g) ripe, firm plum tomatoes, seeded, diced

4 tsp (20 mL) chopped fresh oregano

1 tsp (5 mL) salt

1/2 tsp (2 mL) freshly ground pepper

1 cup (250 mL) grated Pecorino Romano cheese

1/2 lb (250 g) smoked mozzarella cheese, sliced

Preheat the oven to 400°F (200°C). In a large mixing bowl, combine half of the olive oil with the potatoes, garlic, onions, tomatoes, oregano, salt, pepper and half of the Pecorino Romano cheese. Use your hands to mix the ingredients well. Lightly grease an 11- × 7-inch (2 L) baking dish with a little of the oil. Place the potato mixture in the dish, drizzle with the remaining olive oil and sprinkle with the remaining Pecorino Romano cheese.

Cover the dish with foil, making sure that the foil does not touch the cheese. Bake for 45 minutes, remove the foil and distribute the mozzarella slices over the surface of the potatoes. Return the dish to the oven for another 15 minutes, or until the cheese is bubbly and brown. Use the broiler for the last 5 minutes if necessary.

Warm Potato & Mussel Salad with Lemon & Saffron

MAKES 6 SERVINGS

FOR THE MUSSELS:

4 lbs (2 kg) fresh mussels

2 cloves garlic, crushed

3 tbsp (45 mL) olive oil

6 stalks flat-leaf parsley

2 cups (500 mL) dry white wine

Salt and freshly ground pepper

FOR THE POTATOES:

2 lbs (1 kg) small red-skinned potatoes

Salt

3 tbsp (45 mL) extra virgin olive oil

Juice of 1 large lemon

Salt and freshly ground pepper

2 tbsp (30 mL) cold butter

1/2 tsp (2 mL) saffron

2 tbsp (30 mL) chopped fresh parsley

This lovely starter reminds me of Ireland and northern Spain as each of these places are renowned for both great potatoes and wonderfully meaty mussels. Serve this salad with lots of good, crusty bread to soak up the buttery sauce.

Start by soaking the mussels in cold water, changing the water once or twice. Discard any mussels that have broken shells, float or don't close when tapped. Scrub the mussels clean under running water and debeard them. Sauté the garlic in the olive oil in a large skillet or other pan large enough to hold the mussels. After a minute or two, add the parsley stalks, wine, salt and pepper and all of the mussels. Cover the pan, increase the heat and cook, shaking the pan frequently, for about 2 minutes. Transfer any mussels that have opened to a large bowl, discarding the empty half of their shell. Replace the cover on the pan and continue cooking, shaking the pan and removing the cooked mussels. Repeat the process and discard any mussels that don't open. Strain the liquid through a fine sieve into a small saucepan and reserve.

Cook the potatoes in boiling, lightly salted water until tender. Drain and slice them thinly into a bowl. In another bowl, whisk together the oil, lemon juice and salt and pepper and pour the mixture over the warm potatoes. Add the dressed potatoes to the mussels in their bowl. Warm the reserved mussel liquid and whisk in the cold butter. When it begins to froth, add the saffron, whisk once or twice and pour the butter mixture over the potatoes and mussels. Sprinkle with parsley and serve at once.

Spinach & Potato Gnocchi

I like to serve these rich little dumplings with just a gloss of melted butter, a squirt of lemon and freshly ground pepper. If you want to go the extra distance, however, make a simple little tomato sauce or Gorgonzola cream sauce, either one of which will work very well with the gnocchi.

MAKES 4 TO 6 SERVINGS

1 1/2 lbs (750 g) fresh spinach

1 1/2 lbs (750 g) boiling potatoes, scrubbed, halved

1 tsp (5 mL) salt

2 1/2 cups (625 mL) all-purpose flour (approx.)

2 eggs

1 tsp (5 mL) salt

1/4 cup (60 mL) melted butter

Juice of 1 lemon

Salt and freshly ground pepper

Trim and wash the spinach. Place it in a large saucepan with just the water that clings to the leaves after washing. Cook, covered, over high heat until steam begins to escape from beneath the lid. Remove the lid, toss the spinach and cook 1 minute longer, or until tender. Drain, pressing the spinach against the sides of the colander to squeeze out as much water as possible. Cool slightly. Chop the spinach finely and set aside.

Place the potatoes in a large saucepan. Add cold water to cover and sprinkle in the 1 teaspoon (5 mL) salt. Bring to a boil, reduce the heat and simmer the potatoes until they are tender. Drain and return them to the pot. Reduce the heat and cook the potatoes, shaking the pan occasionally, for 1 minute, or until surface moisture has evaporated. When cool enough to handle, remove the skins and mash the potatoes roughly.

In a food processor, combine the potatoes and spinach; pulse on and off just until blended. (Alternatively, stir together by hand in a large bowl, or put through a food mill until blended.) Turn the mixture out onto a clean work surface.

Using your hands, gently work in about 1/2 cup (125 mL) of the flour. Work in
1 egg, then another 1/2 cup (125 mL) flour. Work in the remaining egg, followed by 1/2 cup (125 mL) flour. Work in just enough of the remaining flour to
keep the dough from sticking. Try not to knead the gnocchi dough longer than a
few minutes; the less you handle the gnocchi, the lighter they will be. When the
dough is smooth, divide it into 3 parts.

On a lightly floured board, roll each piece of dough into a sausage shape, about
3/4 inch (1 cm) in diameter. Use about 1 inch (2.5 cm) of dough to make each
gnocchi, shaping the dough into a little elongated oval. Transfer the gnocchi to a
baking sheet lined with waxed paper, spacing them well apart so that they don't
stick to each other. (Gnocchi can be made to this point several hours ahead of time;
cover them with plastic wrap and store in the refrigerator until ready to cook.)

Cook the gnocchi in boiling, lightly salted water in batches of 20 for about
4 minutes. Transfer them to a warmed mixing bowl, toss with melted butter,
lemon juice and salt and pepper. Serve immediately.

Dad's Champion Champ

In my introduction I talked about the significance of this dish in my house when I was growing up. My Dad was born in Belfast and this was one of his favourite meals, especially when served with a soft-boiled egg served in its centre as my Mum was wont to do. Comfort and joy in one easy dish.

2 lbs (1 kg) floury potatoes, peeled
1 tsp (5 mL) salt
2/3 cup (150 mL) whole milk
5 green onions, finely chopped

4 soft-boiled eggs (optional)
1/4 cup (60 mL) butter
Salt and freshly ground pepper

Cut the potatoes into even chunks and cover with cold water, add the 1 teaspoon (5 mL) salt and bring to a boil. Cook the potatoes for about 20 minutes or until tender. While the potatoes cook, warm the milk in a saucepan over gentle heat, add the onions, bring to a boil, reduce the heat and simmer for a few minutes until the onions are tender. (If you plan to serve the champ with soft-boiled eggs, put 4 large eggs in a saucepan, cover them with water and bring to a boil; remove from the heat and let stand for 4 minutes.)

Drain the potatoes, return them to low heat and shake the pan over the element for a minute or so to make sure they are quite dry. Mash the potatoes with the milk mixture and butter until smooth. Season with salt and pepper. Cover the potatoes with a clean tea towel and the saucepan lid while you shell the eggs. Spoon the potato into 4 warmed pasta bowls, make a well in the centre of the potatoes, place an egg in the well, slice the egg in half and add more salt and pepper, if desired. Serve immediately.

Brandade with Toasted Pita

1 lb (500 g) salt cod, soaked

2 1/2 cups (625 mL) whole milk

1 bay leaf

3 large floury potatoes, peeled

Salt

3 cloves garlic

1/2 bunch flat-leaf parsley

Juice of 1 large lemon

Freshly ground pepper

1 cup (250 mL) extra virgin olive oil

6 pita breads

Olive oil

This savoury brandade—an appetizer of salt cod blended with potato and olive oil—is rich, smooth and satisfying, and the crisped pita breads provide just the right textural contrast.

To soften and desalinate the salt cod, immerse it in cold water and soak overnight, changing the water two or three times.

Break the cod into chunks and place them in a large saucepan. Add the milk, bay leaf and, if necessary, enough water so that the fish is submerged in liquid. Bring to a gentle boil and poach the fish for about 15 minutes, or until it is cooked and falls apart easily. Use a slotted spoon to transfer the fish to a bowl to cool. When the fish has cooled, remove and discard any skin and bones. Reserve the poaching liquid.

Bring another saucepan of water to a boil and cook the potatoes with a little salt. When cooked, drain and leave to cool.

Crush the garlic with the broad side of a chef's knife. Remove the stems from the parsley and roughly chop the leaves. Place the fish and potatoes in the bowl of a food processor. Add the garlic, parsley, lemon juice and a little pepper. Process on high while adding about 1/4 cup (60 mL) of the reserved poaching liquid. While the processor is still running, slowly the add olive oil in a thin stream until the mixture has reached a smooth, spreadable consistency. Preheat the oven to 400°F (200°C). Brush the pitas with a little olive oil, place them on a baking sheet and bake them until they begin to crisp up around the edges; alternatively, brush the pitas with oil and toast them in a hot skillet until crisped. Transfer the brandade to a serving bowl and serve with crisped pitas alongside.

When the need for true comfort strikes, nothing works quite as well as an unabashedly sumptuous potato preparation. It doesn't have to be fancy, fiddly or upscale; it can be as simple as soft potato dumplings or new potatoes sautéed with garlic, or as traditional as the Irish classic *colcannon*. With potatoes in the house, comfort is close at hand.

the comforting potato

Potato Dumplings with Chicken & Tarragon Cream

MAKES 4 TO 6 SERVINGS

Chicken and dumplings pack a lot of comfort into one simple dish. This version gussies things up a bit by using chicken breasts with a little cream and fresh tarragon. Then everything is topped with the lightest, fluffiest potato dumplings ever. These dumplings will also work well with a beef or lamb stew, or make them a little smaller and float them atop a sturdy vegetable soup. Prepare the cooked potatoes for the dumplings ahead of time.

FOR THE CHICKEN:

1 1/2 cups (375 mL) chicken broth
1 cup (250 mL) dry white wine
6 black peppercorns
3 stalks fresh flat-leaf parsley
1 onion, chopped
1 stalk celery, chopped
4 large chicken breasts
1 1/4 cups (300 mL) table cream
2 tbsp (30 mL) chopped fresh tarragon
Salt and freshly ground pepper

FOR THE DUMPLINGS:

6 medium floury potatoes, peeled,
    boiled, mashed
2 large eggs
1/2 cup (125 mL) all-purpose flour
1 1/2 tsp (7 mL) salt
2 tbsp (30 mL) chopped fresh
    flat-leaf parsley

Combine the chicken broth, wine, peppercorns, parsley stalks, onion and celery in a large skillet. Place the chicken breasts in the mixture, bring to a gentle boil, reduce the heat immediately and simmer for about 20 minutes, loosely covered. Using tongs, transfer the chicken breasts to a cutting board and let them cool slightly. Strain the cooking liquid, discarding the solids, and return it to the skillet. Discard the chicken skin and bones and pull the meat apart into rough chunks. Increase the heat and gently boil the cooking liquid to reduce it slightly—not too much, just enough to thicken it a bit. Stir in the cream and tarragon and season with salt and pepper. Place the chicken pieces in a 4-cup (1 L) baking dish. Pour the sauce over the chicken. Set the chicken to one side as you prepare the dumpling mixture.

Preheat the oven to 375°F (190°C). Combine the mashed potatoes with the eggs, flour and salt, beating the mixture until it is fairly fluffy. Lightly flour your hands and shape the mixture into 1-inch (2.5 cm) balls. Make enough dumplings to cover the chicken, pushing them down into the sauce to partially submerge them. (If you have more than enough dumplings, place them in another baking dish, add a little more chicken broth and cook them at the same time as the main dish.) Bake the chicken and dumplings, uncovered, for 25 to 30 minutes. Serve immediately.

 No garden space for spuds? Grow them in a large container like a halved wooden barrel. Put six inches of soil in the barrel and plant three seed potatoes, evenly spaced. Cover them with about four inches of soil. When you first spot some foliage, add more soil so that just the green tips are showing. As the potatoes grow, continue to add more soil until the soil level is about two inches from the rim of the barrel. Water and fertilize the plants regularly, and harvest your potatoes when the foliage starts to turn yellow and brown.

Potato Pancakes with Cinnamon Apples & Yogurt Cheese

MAKES 4 SERVINGS

You can make a series of pancakes with this recipe or one giant pancake, as I sometimes like to do, cutting it into pie-shaped wedges to serve. I've made this dish with floury, all-purpose and even waxy potatoes (with the latter you have to try a little harder to keep the shreds together), and it is unfailingly great every time. Be careful with the amount of flour; using too much will make the cakes leaden. If you make this dish for breakfast, serve it with back bacon, or omit the apples and serve it with poached or fried eggs on top.

Yogurt cheese is simply thick, plain yogurt that has been allowed to drain for at least 6 hours or, preferably, overnight.

FOR THE YOGURT CHEESE:
2 cups (500 mL) whole-milk yogurt

FOR THE PANCAKES:
1 lb (500 kg) floury potatoes, peeled
1 small onion
3 eggs, lightly beaten
2–3 tbsp (30–45 mL) all-purpose flour
Salt and freshly ground pepper
1/4 cup (60 mL) butter
1/4 cup (60 mL) olive oil

FOR THE CINNAMON APPLES:
Half a lemon
3 McIntosh apples, peeled, cored, sliced
1/2 tsp (2 mL) cinnamon
1/2 tsp (2 mL) nutmeg
1 tbsp (15 mL) dark brown sugar

To make the yogurt cheese, spoon the yogurt into a paper coffee filter. Place the filter in a sieve or strainer set over a deep bowl. Cover with plastic wrap and let the yogurt drain in the fridge overnight. Discard the liquid. Transfer the yogurt cheese to a covered container and refrigerate until ready to use.

For the pancakes, coarsely grate the potatoes over a mixing bowl. Place the grated potatoes on a clean tea towel. Gather up the towel and wring it out over the sink to remove as much water from the potatoes as possible. Grate the onion.

Wipe the bowl clean and beat the eggs in it. Add the potato, onion and half the flour; season with salt and pepper. Blend all the ingredients together with a fork and add some of the remaining flour if necessary. If the mixture looks quite wet, add a little more or all of the remaining flour. Heat some of the butter and oil in a large, heavy skillet over medium-high heat. When the fat is quite hot, drop spoonfuls of the potato mixture into the pan and, using a spatula, gently flatten each cake slightly to a thickness of about 1/4 inch (5 mm). Cook and brown the pancakes on one side, flip them and cook on the other side, about 3 minutes per side. Use more butter and oil for subsequent batches as needed, allowing the fat to get quite hot before adding the potato mixture. (Reserve a little of the butter and oil for sautéing the apples.) Keep the cooked pancakes warm in a low oven.

Squeeze the lemon over the apples. Mix the apples with the juice to prevent them from browning. Wipe the skillet clean, add the remaining butter and oil and, when the butter has melted, add the apple slices, cinnamon and nutmeg. Sauté the apple slices for a few minutes. Add the brown sugar and continue to cook for a few minutes longer, until the apple slices start to glaze a bit; don't cook the apple so much that it becomes totally soft. Serve the pancakes with the glazed apples and yogurt cheese.

Potato Nest Eggs
with Bacon & Cheddar

MAKES 2 TO 4 SERVINGS

Once baked and hollowed out, a big baked potato provides a great vehicle for so many good things: mushrooms, asparagus pieces, sun-dried tomatoes, smoked fish, ham or salami, a variety of cheeses and fresh herbs. Think of this recipe as just the starting point. It's great for a brunch or late-night bite.

4 large floury baking potatoes, scrubbed
1/4 cup (60 mL) butter
4–6 strips bacon, cooked, crumbled
1 cup (250 mL) grated old Cheddar cheese
1/4 cup (60 mL) chopped fresh chives or finely chopped green onions
Salt and freshly ground pepper
4 eggs

Preheat the oven to 400°F (200°C). Bake the potatoes for 1 hour (a little longer if they are very large) until cooked through. Let them cool slightly.

Using a small, sharp knife, cut a lid-like section lengthwise across each potato. Set the lids aside and, with a small spoon, carefully scoop as much of the flesh out of the potatoes as you can, placing it in a bowl. When all the potatoes have been hollowed out, add butter to the potato flesh and mash well. Add the bacon, cheese and chives or green onions to the mixture and combine well. Season with salt and pepper.

Spoon this mixture into the potatoes, distributing it evenly among them and pressing it down to form a well for the egg. Place the potatoes in a baking dish. Crack an egg into the hollow in each potato, top with the reserved lid and bake for about 10 to 13 minutes, or until the eggs are cooked to your liking. Serve immediately.

Sautéed Fingerlings with Asparagus & Mint

MAKES 4 TO 6 SERVINGS

1 1/2 lbs (750 g) fingerling potatoes,
   scrubbed
Salt
1 lb (500 g) thin asparagus, trimmed

2 tbsp (30 mL) butter
2 tbsp (30 mL) olive oil
15 fresh mint leaves
Salt and freshly ground pepper

Cover the whole potatoes with boiling water, add a little salt and boil until the potatoes are almost cooked through, about 12 minutes. Drain. When the potatoes are cool enough to handle, slice them lengthwise into thick slices. Slice the asparagus on an angle into thirds. Heat the butter and olive oil in a heavy skillet until hot. Add the potatoes and asparagus and cook until the potatoes are golden brown and the asparagus is tender. Add the mint leaves and salt and pepper and toss with the potatoes and asparagus. Serve immediately.

This is a lovely dish to make whenever you spy these special new potatoes in your area. Fingerlings are long, knobby potatoes with a wonderfully smooth, waxy texture and much flavour. They are stylish enough to serve with the season's first asparagus; choose those pencil-thin stalks for this dish. If the asparagus is thicker, blanch it in boiling water for a minute before adding to potatoes.

Chips in Curry Sauce

Strictly an Anglo invention, this is the ultimate antidote after a pub crawl. It may sound an unlikely combination until you realize just how fond of curry people are in the U.K. It was only a matter of time before someone over 'ome put these two favourites together and I, for one, am very glad they did.

Put the sauce together first, then make the recipe for English Chips on page 30. This curry sauce recipe makes about 3 cups (750 mL) of sauce and it will keep for about 3 to 4 days covered and refrigerated. You'll find lots of other uses for it, too. If you really want to go over the top, serve the chips in sauce rolled up in an Indian bread like paratha or chapati—the curried chip butty!

MAKES 4 SERVINGS

1 tsp (5 mL) unsalted butter

1 small onion, chopped

Salt

2 tbsp (30 mL) all-purpose flour

2 cloves garlic, minced

1 large Northern Spy or Golden Delicious apple, cored, peeled, chopped

1 medium ripe tomato, chopped

3 cups (750 mL) chicken stock

1 cup (250 mL) light unsweetened coconut milk (sold in cans; shake can well before opening)

1/4 cup (60 mL) ground almonds

4–5 tbsp (60–75 mL) curry powder

2 tbsp (30 mL) chopped fresh gingerroot

1 tsp (5 mL) tomato paste

Melt the butter in a large saucepan over medium-high heat. Sauté the onion with a little salt for a few minutes until softened. Add the flour and stir well into the mixture, continuing to cook for another couple of minutes. Now add the garlic, apple, tomato, chicken stock, coconut milk, ground almonds, curry powder, gingerroot and tomato paste. Stir everything together to combine well. Cover loosely and simmer slowly for 1 hour and 30 minutes, or until the mixture has thickened and the flavour has developed. Transfer the mixture to a food processor and purée (in batches, if necessary) until smooth. When the chips are ready, serve immediately with this sauce either on the side or lavishly poured over the chips.

Maxwell's All-Ireland Champion Fries

MAKES 4 TO 6 SERVINGS

4 large baking potatoes, scrubbed

2 cups (500 mL) all-purpose flour

1 tbsp (15 mL) cayenne pepper

1 tsp (5 mL) freshly ground pepper

1 tsp (5 mL) salt

2 cups (500 mL) buttermilk

Vegetable oil

Preheat the oven to 425°F (220°C). Place the potatoes in the centre of the oven and bake for 1 hour. While they are baking, combine the flour, cayenne, pepper and salt in a shallow bowl and mix well. Pour the buttermilk into another shallow bowl and set to one side. Remove the potatoes from the oven and allow them to cool. Slice each potato in half lengthwise, then slice each half lengthwise into 4 strips. Dip the potatoes into the buttermilk and then dredge them in the seasoned flour. Repeat the process for a second coating and transfer the potatoes to a parchment paper–lined baking sheet. Loosely cover them with plastic wrap and let sit for 6 hours. (They do not have to be refrigerated.) When you are ready to cook the potatoes, heat the oil in a deep-fryer or similar heavy pot to 365°F (185°C). If you are not using a deep-fryer, use a candy thermometer to gauge the temperature of the oil. Deep-fry the potatoes until crisp and golden brown on all sides, about 3 minutes in total. Serve immediately.

The lovely wooded bar/restaurant known as Allen's is an institution on Danforth Avenue, in the east end of Toronto. Allen's is renowned for so many good things: food, ale, spirits—and spirit, most of which emanates from owner John Maxwell, who I am blessed to be able to describe as my good friend. I have devoured many a plate of spuds at Allen's, whether in the form of their famous "half and half" (sweet potato and white potato fries) or these honking great beauties. A great Guinness go-with. Good for what "ales" ya! Serve with sour cream blended with fresh chives.

Spiced Potato Ribbon Chips

MAKES 6 SERVINGS

I purposely did not place this recipe in The Appetizing Potato section because these chips, and the Garlic Saratogas that follow, are too good to share ... well, with more than one or two true-blue buddies anyway. These are for you and your favourite couch potato to enjoy along with a few quality beers and an old black and white movie. Choose the longest baking potatoes you can find for this recipe. Pick up a container of good quality tzatziki to serve alongside as a cooling dip.

4 cups (1 L) ice water

1 tbsp (15 mL) + 1 tsp (5 mL) salt

6 large baking potatoes, scrubbed

Vegetable oil as needed

1 tbsp (15 mL) chili powder

1/2 tsp (2 mL) cayenne pepper

Have the ice water ready in a large bowl. Add the 1 tablespoon (15 mL) salt to the water and give it a good stir. Then, using a vegetable peeler, peel lengthwise strips from the potatoes, allowing the strips to fall into the ice water as you work. Let the potato strips sit in the ice water as you heat the oil to 375°F (190°C) in a deep-fryer or heavy pan. If you are not using a deep-fryer, use a candy thermometer to gauge the temperature of the oil. Warm the oven.

In a small bowl, combine the chili powder, 1 teaspoon (5 mL) salt and cayenne; mix together well. Drain the potatoes and pat dry thoroughly. Fry the potatoes in small batches until crisp and golden, transferring them to a paper towel–lined baking sheet. Keep the chips warm in the oven as you cook subsequent batches. When all the chips have been made, sprinkle on the spice mixture and serve immediately.

Garlic Saratogas

4 cups (1 L) ice water

6 large baking potatoes, peeled

Vegetable oil

2 cloves garlic, pressed

3 tbsp (45 mL) butter

2 tbsp (30 mL) very finely chopped
    flat-leaf parsley

Salt and freshly ground pepper

Warm the oven. Have ready the ice water in a large bowl. Slice the potatoes very thinly and place the slices in the ice water as you work. Heat the oil in a deep-fryer or heavy pan to 325°F (160°C). If you are not using a deep-fryer, use a candy thermometer to gauge the temperature of the oil. Drain the potatoes and run cold water over them. When the water runs clear, dry the potato slices thoroughly. In three batches, carefully add them to the hot oil and fry until they are light brown and crisp. Jostle the chips around a little with a slotted spoon to encourage even cooking. Remove the chips with the slotted spoon as they are done and place them on a paper towel–lined baking sheet. Keep them warm in the oven.

When all the potatoes have been fried, combine the garlic and butter in a small saucepan over medium heat. Don't let the garlic brown. Pile the potato chips in a large serving bowl, drizzle with the butter and garlic mixture, add the parsley and season with salt and pepper. Very gently turn the chips with a rubber spatula to coat them with the seasonings. Serve hot.

Saratoga chips are so named because they were invented by a chef named George Crum—if you can believe it—in Saratoga Springs, New York, in 1853. Not long after that, you could find vendors selling paper cones filled with warm potato chips all over New York City—oh to have lived there then! This version treats those remarkable chips to a little garlic and seasoning, rather like the wonderful potato chips chef Chris McDonald makes from time to time at Avalon, his terrific restaurant in Toronto. You'll notice that the oil temperature is lower than for the Spiced Potato Ribbon Chips. This is so that the chips can cook longer and really crisp up. It's not vital, but a mandoline will make slicing the potatoes easier; the slices should be about 1/16-inch (1.5 mm) thick. Use a garlic press for the garlic.

Spud & Onion Stuffing

MAKES ENOUGH FOR A 12-POUND (5.5 KG) TURKEY

You could also use this moist, flavourful stuffing with boneless pork loin or whole chicken breasts. A friend of mine uses it to fill large portobello mushroom caps before baking! Very easy and very good.

4 cups (1 L) hot, homemade
   mashed potatoes
2 eggs, lightly beaten
1/2 cup (125 mL) butter
1 cup (250 mL) chopped onion
6 cups (1.5 L) dry bread cubes

1/2 cup (125 mL) chopped fresh chives
1/2 cup (125 mL) chopped fresh
   flat-leaf parsley
2 tsp (10 mL) freshly ground pepper
2 tsp (10 mL) salt

In a mixing bowl, combine the potatoes with the eggs. Melt the butter in a skillet and sauté the onion until softened. Cool slightly and scrape the onion into the bowl containing the potatoes. Add all the remaining ingredients and mix well. If the mixture seems dry, add a little more melted butter or a drizzle or two of good olive oil.

Pot Roast Crusties

MAKES 8 SERVINGS

2 lbs (1 kg) small red-skinned potatoes,
    scrubbed

1/2 cup (125 mL) olive oil

1 cup (250 mL) dry breadcrumbs

2 tbsp (30 mL) paprika

2 tsp (10 mL) herbes de Provence

Salt and freshly ground pepper

Preheat the oven to 350°F (180°C). Halve the potatoes and place them in a large mixing bowl. Cover the potatoes with the olive oil and toss to coat them well. Add the breadcrumbs, paprika, and herbes de Provence and season with salt and pepper. Toss well to ensure that the breadcrumb mixture coats the potatoes. Line a roasting pan with parchment paper. Using tongs so as not to disturb the coating, place the potatoes one by one on the paper. Roast the potatoes until they are cooked through and a crisp crust has formed, about 50 minutes. Serve immediately.

I call these pot roast potatoes because they go so well with a nice, traditional pot roast of beef. But don't let that stop you from serving them with roast pork or lamb or a big, shiny ham.

Buttered Bubble & Squeak

MAKES 4 TO 6 SERVINGS

3 tbsp (45 mL) butter

3 tbsp (45 mL) olive oil

4 green onions, finely chopped

2 cups (500 mL) cooked cabbage,
   regular or savoy

3 cups (750 mL) mashed potatoes

Salt and freshly ground pepper

Butter

Named for the sounds that emanate from it as it cooks, this Irish dish is known in that country as colcannon *and is a tradition on All Hallows Eve—Halloween—which is the ancient Celtic New Year's Eve. Often little charms would be added to this dish for children to discover. Some maintain that true bubble and squeak contains meat while* colcannon *does not. Either way, it makes a lovely comforting dish, perfect to serve alongside good quality sausages. This is one dish that, I maintain, should be made with leftover mashed potato and cabbage; somehow it's not as good when the central ingredients are freshly made. One Sunday morning, my husband shaped some of this mixture into patties and fried them with a little double-smoked bacon. Leftover leftovers never tasted so good.*

Heat the butter and olive oil in a large heavy skillet over medium-high heat. Add the onion and cook until softened, a few minutes. Add the cabbage and toss with the onion. Add the potatoes to the pan, breaking them up roughly with a fork as you combine them with the cabbage mixture. Season with salt and pepper. When the potatoes are heated through, transfer to a warmed serving dish. Make a well in the centre of the bubble and squeak and add a big knob of butter to melt as you serve.

Skillet Potato Galette

2 tbsp (30 mL) butter

2 cloves garlic, minced

2 large onions, sliced 1/4-inch (5 mm) thick

2 lbs (1 kg) small red-skinned potatoes,
   scrubbed, sliced 1/4-inch (5 mm) thick

3 tbsp (45 mL) olive oil

Salt and freshly ground pepper

1 cup (250 mL) shredded Jarlsberg cheese

1/4 cup (60 mL) chopped fresh
   flat-leaf parsley

Melt the butter in a large heavy skillet and sauté the garlic and onion for about 5 minutes. Add the potato and olive oil and season with salt and pepper, mixing the ingredients thoroughly. Cook for about 10 minutes, tossing the potatoes around to brown them on both sides. Cover, reduce the heat a little and cook for another 10 minutes or so until the potatoes are tender.

Combine the cheese and parsley, sprinkle the mixture over the potatoes and continue cooking until the cheese has melted. Serve immediately.

Not a galette in the true sense of the term (see page 88 for the real thing), this dish is sort of a cross between home fries and a gratin. It is an easy preparation that requires minimum effort but provides much comfort eating.

Yukon Gold
Bay Leaf Mash

This recipe is from chef Stephen Treadwell of the Tiara dining room, Queen's Landing Inn, Niagara-on-the-Lake. At the restaurant, Treadwell pairs this simple, yet sumptuous side dish with maple roasted salmon and a reduction of Cabernet Sauvignon and mustard seed. Use the very best extra virgin olive oil for this recipe.

MAKES 2 TO 4 SERVINGS

1 cup (250 mL) extra virgin olive oil
3–4 bay leaves, crushed
4–5 large Yukon Gold potatoes, baked

1/4 cup (60 mL) chopped fresh parsley
Salt and freshly ground pepper

Warm the olive oil in a small sauté pan. Pour the oil over the crushed bay leaf, cover with plastic wrap and allow to infuse for 1 hour. When the potatoes are cool enough to handle, spoon the flesh out of the skins into a bowl. Keep the potato flesh warm. Strain the olive oil and add it with the parsley, roughly incorporating into the potato. Season with salt and pepper. Serve immediately.

It took many years for certain cultures to fully accept the potato as a staple of their diet. Even the poorest, hungriest and most destitute, suspicious of the root, had to be forcefully convinced. In Russia in the early 1800s, the government firmly ordered peasants to plant crops of potatoes, an edict that was met with uprisings, battles and riots in 10 communities.

Lemon Spice Spuds

FOR THE GARAM MASALA:

2-inch (5 cm) cinnamon stick

1/3 whole nutmeg

1 tbsp (15 mL) cardamom seeds

1 tsp (5 mL) whole black peppercorns

1 tsp (5 mL) whole black cumin seeds

1 tsp (5 mL) whole cloves

1 tsp (5 mL) whole mustard seeds

FOR THE POTATOES:

2 lbs (1 kg) floury potatoes, scrubbed

Salt

1/2 cup (125 mL) extra virgin olive oil

2 tbsp (30 mL) garam masala

1 tbsp (15 mL) turmeric

3 cloves garlic, minced

1 tbsp (15 mL) chopped fresh gingerroot

Zest and juice of 1 large lemon

Salt and freshly ground pepper

To make the garam masala, place all of the ingredients in a clean coffee grinder and grind to a fine powder. Set aside.

Cut the potatoes into rough chunks and place them in a saucepan. Just cover with cold water, add a little salt, bring to a boil and cook for about 6 minutes. Drain the potatoes and place them in a bowl to cool.

Preheat the oven to 400°F (200°C). Using the tines of a fork, rough up the edges of the potatoes. In a large heavy skillet, warm the olive oil. As it is warming, toss the potatoes in the garam masala and the turmeric. Add the potatoes to the oil, along with the garlic, gingerroot, lemon zest and juice. Season with salt and pepper. Toss the potatoes around to coat them well with all the ingredients. Using a rubber spatula, transfer the potatoes to a roasting pan, making sure to include all the oil and spice mixture. Roast the potatoes for about 1 hour until crusty and golden brown.

This preparation is inspired by Greek-style potatoes treated with lemon and olive oil to which I have added some fragrant Indian ingredients, making them even better. Serve them with seared lamb chops and skinny green beans. Garam masala is a group of Indian seasonings, the phrase translating as "hot spices." In India the actual spices used vary with each household, but the mix usually includes cardamom, cloves, cumin, cinnamon and nutmeg. Look for garam masala in specialty food shops or Indian grocery stores, or make your own with this classic combination that you can vary according to your taste. This may make a little more than you require for this recipe. Store any remaining garam masala in a little jar with a tight-fitting lid and keep in a dark, dry place.

Pasta with Taleggio, Potatoes & Cabbage

MAKES 6 SERVINGS

Very good for whatever might ail you on a cold, wintry night, this is a true one-dish supper. Be careful not to overcook the pasta as it will be cooked a little more in the oven at the end.

3 Yukon Gold potatoes, peeled, cut into small chunks

1 tsp (5 mL) coarse salt

1 lb (500 g) fettuccine

8 oz (250 g) savoy cabbage, halved, cored, cut into strips (approx. 1/2 head)

3 tbsp (45 mL) butter

12 sage leaves, torn into pieces

6 cloves garlic, thinly sliced

Salt and freshly ground pepper

1 cup (250 mL) grated Parmigiano-Reggiano cheese

10 oz (300 g) Taleggio cheese, diced

Bring a large pot of water to a boil. Stir in the potatoes and coarse salt. Reduce the heat to medium-high and cook the potatoes for 3 minutes, or until they are softened but not cooked through. Stir in the pasta and cabbage, increase the heat to high and cook for 8 minutes, or until the pasta is not quite tender. Drain, reserving about 1 cup (250 mL) of the cooking liquid. Return the pasta and vegetables to the pot and set aside. Preheat the oven to 450°F (230°C).

Melt the butter in a skillet over medium-low heat. Add the sage and garlic and season with salt and pepper. Cook for 3 minutes, or until the garlic is softened but not browned. Pour the sage mixture over the pasta and vegetables, along with all but a heaping tablespoon (15 mL) of the Parmigiano-Reggiano. Toss the ingredients together gently. Put one-third of the mixture into lightly buttered 3-quart (3 L) casserole dish and top with one-third of the Taleggio cheese. Repeat the process, forming 2 more layers. Sprinkle with the reserved Parmigiano-Reggiano. Pour enough of the reserved cooking liquid over top to moisten slightly. Bake in the top half of the oven for 7 minutes, or until the cheese is melted. Let sit for 5 minutes before serving.

Bistro Sausage
& Potato Salad

MAKES 4 TO 6 SERVINGS

FOR THE VINAIGRETTE:

3 tbsp (45 mL) Dijon mustard

3 tbsp (45 mL) lemon juice or white wine
vinegar

3/4 cup extra virgin olive oil

Salt and freshly ground pepper

FOR THE SALAD:

4 large waxy white potatoes

Salt

1 1/2 lbs (750 g) garlic sausage coil

2 heads assorted lettuce (red leaf, Boston,
green leaf), rinsed, dried and separated

1 white onion, thinly sliced

4 ripe plum tomatoes, quartered

6 or 8 gherkins

This is a great little supper to put together when you are hungrier than you are energetic. It's the sort of satisfying, rustic preparation enjoyed by interesting looking people in Parisian bistros who happily dine solo. Look for good quality, lean, garlicky sausage for this dish. Serve the salad with fresh baguette and a good, sturdy red from the south of France.

Prepare the vinaigrette by whisking together the mustard and lemon juice or vinegar in a bowl. Add the olive oil in a thin stream as you continue to whisk. When the vinaigrette is smooth, season with salt and pepper. Set to one side.

Scrub the potatoes, place them in a pot and cover them with boiling water. Bring to a boil, add a bit of salt, reduce the heat and cook slowly until the potatoes are tender, about 30 minutes (as potatoes are left whole, they take a little longer to cook than cut potatoes). Drain the potatoes, cover them with a clean tea towel and a lid and keep them warm.

Prick the sausage a few times and place it in a saucepan with a little water to cover. Bring to a boil, reduce the heat and simmer the sausage for about 20 minutes. Drain the sausage and set to one side to cool.

On a large serving platter, arrange the lettuce leaves and scatter the onion over them. Slice the sausage, not too thickly, and arrange the slices over the greens along with slices of warm potato. Add the tomatoes and gherkins on the side. Drizzle the vinaigrette over the salad and serve.

Potato Fritters
with Salmon & Dill

I devised these little fritters one day when I found myself with leftover cooked salmon fillets that my husband had smoked in our backyard smoker. You can fill these delectable little fritters with anything you like—tuna, chicken, ground beef, cheese or ham. While you make them with leftover mashed potato, I think they are at their best when prepared with fresh "dry" mash; that is, potatoes mashed just on their own without the addition of butter or milk. These fritters are great for dinner served with wedges of lemon and tartar sauce or piquant chili sauce and a big green salad, or make them a little smaller and serve them as hors d'oeuvres.

MAKES 6 SERVINGS

2 lbs (1 kg) floury baking potatoes, peeled
Salt
3 eggs, separated
1/2 tsp (2 mL) lemon herb seasoning
1/4 cup (60 mL) finely chopped fresh dill
Salt and freshly ground pepper

1 cup (250 mL) fine dry breadcrumbs
Olive oil or other vegetable oil
1 cup (250 mL) cooked salmon fillet, cut into
   pieces (you can use canned, drained
   salmon but try to keep the pieces
   fairly intact)

Put the potatoes in a large saucepan, cover them with cold water, bring to a boil, add a little salt and cook over medium heat until the potatoes are soft, about 25 minutes. Drain thoroughly, shake the potatoes in the pan over low heat for a minute or so to completely dry them and mash them until smooth. Set to one side to cool slightly. When cooled, beat the egg yolks into the potatoes, one at a time, add the lemon herb seasoning and the dill and season with salt and pepper, mixing all the ingredients together well. In a bowl, whisk the egg whites together until frothy. Set to one side.

Scatter the breadcrumbs onto a plate. Use a bit of the oil to grease your hands so that the potato mixture doesn't stick to them as you make the fritters. Shape about 1/4 cup (60 mL) of the potato mixture into a ball and make a well in the centre of it. Fill the well with a piece of salmon and cup the potato mixture up and around the filling to enclose it. Dip the potato ball into the egg white and then the bread-crumbs. Place the potato ball on a baking sheet covered with waxed or parchment paper and repeat the process with the remaining ingredients.

Pour oil into a deep, heavy skillet to a depth of about 2 inches (5 cm). Place the skillet over fairly high heat. Use a candy thermometer to gauge when the oil has reached 350°F (180°C). Carefully add a few fritters to the skillet (don't crowd them) and fry until they are golden brown on all sides, about 3 to 4 minutes. Drain the fritters on paper toweling and serve.

Potato & Porcini Croustade

MAKES 8 SERVINGS

2 oz (60 g) dried porcini

1 cup (250 mL) warm water

3 large floury baking potatoes, peeled

1/2 lb (250 g) assorted mushrooms, wiped
   clean, sliced

4 shallots, finely sliced

3 cloves garlic, finely chopped

2 tbsp (30 mL) chopped fresh
   flat-leaf parsley

1 tsp (5 mL) chopped fresh rosemary

1 tsp (5 mL) chopped fresh thyme

Salt and freshly ground pepper

1/2 lb (250 g) frozen puff pastry
   dough, thawed

1 1/2 cups (375 mL) table cream

Place the dried porcini in a small bowl and cover them with the warm water. Let stand for 1 hour. Strain (reserving the liquid), chop the porcini and set them to one side. Preheat the oven to 400°F (200°C).

Cut the potatoes into 1/4-inch (5 mm) slices. Place them in a large bowl along with the sliced mushrooms and the chopped porcini. Add the shallots, garlic, parsley, rosemary and thyme and season with salt and pepper. Toss the ingredients together well.

On a lightly floured surface, roll out the puff pastry dough to a thickness of about 1/4 inch (5 mm). Place the dough on a nonstick baking sheet. Using your hands, pile the potato mixture in the centre of the pastry, allowing a 3-inch (8 cm) border all around the potato mixture. Now, turn up the edges of the pastry over the filling, overlapping the pastry as necessary and leaving the centre of the filling uncovered. In a bowl, combine 1/2 cup (125 mL) of the reserved mushroom liquid with the cream. Pour this mixture into the centre of the potato mixture in the dough. Carefully place the baking sheet in the oven. Bake the croustade for 20 minutes, reduce the heat to 375°F (190°C) and continue to bake for a further 40 minutes, or until the crust is golden brown and the potatoes are tender. Remove the croustade from the oven and let sit for a few minutes before serving.

If we all lived in Italy's Umbria, we would always be able to get fabulous porcini—fresh and dried. Well, thank goodness for exporters and fine food shops that make sure we in North America have access to these prized fungi. Far from being a poor substitute for fresh porcini, fine quality dried porcini are wonderfully flavourful. When rehydrated, a few ounces go a long way toward making a larger quantity of common mushrooms much more interesting. Use as wide an assortment of mushrooms as possible for this rustic, cold-weather tart.

Gnocchi-roni & Cheese

Here is a recipe for sturdy little potato gnocchi that receive their final cooking combined with a rich cheese sauce in the oven, where they get lovely and splotchy brown like mac and cheese. Everybody goes for this in a big way. Serve with a tomato and avocado salad and crusty bread.

MAKES 4 TO 6 SERVINGS

FOR THE GNOCCHI:
3 floury potatoes, peeled, quartered
Salt
2 eggs, lightly beaten
1 1/2 cups (375 mL) all-purpose flour

FOR THE SAUCE:
2 tbsp (30 mL) butter
1 1/2 tbsp (20 mL) all-purpose flour
1/2 tsp (2 mL) dry mustard
1/4 tsp (1 mL) paprika
Salt and freshly ground pepper
1 cup (250 mL) whole milk
1 cup (250 mL) grated old Cheddar cheese

Place the potatoes in a saucepan, cover them with cold water and bring to a boil. Add a little salt and cook the potatoes until tender, about 25 minutes. Drain, but reserve the cooking water. Transfer the potatoes to a bowl, let cool, add the eggs and mash well. Gradually add the flour and combine with the potato mixture to form a dough; you may not use all the flour or you may need a little more. Turn the dough out onto a lightly floured surface and knead lightly for 2 minutes until smooth.

Divide the dough into 4 pieces and roll each into a long, cylindrical shape. Using the edge of a fork, cut each length into 1-inch (2.5 cm) pieces. Use the tines of the fork to lightly flatten each piece, leaving an impression. Repeat with the remaining dough.

Return the potato cooking water to the heat and add a little more water to it. Bring to a boil and drop each gnocchi into the water; they will sink to the bottom and then rise. Once they rise, let them continue to cook for about 1 minute. Remove the gnocchi with a slotted spoon and drain them on paper toweling. Lightly grease a baking dish and set it to one side while you prepare the sauce.

Discard the gnocchi cooking water and wipe the saucepan clean. Melt the butter over medium heat and whisk in the flour, mustard, paprika and some salt and pepper; cook for about 1 minute. Remove the pan from heat and gradually whisk in the milk. Return the pan to the heat and bring to a gentle boil, whisking all the while. Add the cheese and stir it into the sauce until completely melted. Transfer the gnocchi to a baking dish and cover them with the cheese sauce. Broil beneath a preheated oven broiler for a few minutes, watching carefully, just until the cheese bubbles and begins to brown in places.

 Early Peruvians were experts in sun-drying potatoes, which they then called *tunta*. However, the Incas used an even more advanced preserving technique that involved freezing the potatoes in the snows of the Andes. Once thawed, the potatoes were squeezed until all the bitter juices were removed. After being left to dry thoroughly (which could take a couple of weeks), the desiccated potatoes (called *chuno*) could be stored for long periods and therefore provided a valuable dietary staple when fresh potatoes were out of season.

When dinner becomes special, so do the potatoes, and that's what this chapter is all about. These are the potato dishes to trot out when you want to show off a little or when you want to give the utmost in potato pleasure to a loved one. There are appetizers and hors d'oeuvres, main courses and side dishes, traditional preparations and a handful of contemporary stars that demonstrate beautifully just how timeless the potato is.

the
dinner party
potato

Grande Dame Anna Potatoes

MAKES 4 SERVINGS

Okay, I'll say it: this is the best damn potato recipe in the world. I have no idea who Anna was, but I am eternally grateful to her or whoever it was who introduced the world to this, the most harmonious blend of potato and butter you will ever encounter. Pommes de Terre Anna, as this dish is formally known, holds the very essence of potato flavour. It is traditionally made in a copper pan, but I have decided the cast-iron skillet is the way to go, mostly because I don't own a copper pan. I like to start the cooking process on the top of the stove, as I build the dish in the skillet.

I would happily eat like a vegan sparrow for the whole week if I knew I was sharing this with my beloved on Saturday night with a rare sirloin and a huge rioja.

3–4 large baking potatoes, peeled
3/4 cup (175 mL) butter, melted
Salt and freshly ground pepper

Preheat the oven to 375°F (190°C). Slice the potatoes crosswise very thinly—about 1/8-inch (3 mm) thick—with a sharp chef's knife or on a mandoline. (If you like, at this point you can use a small round cookie cutter to make each circle perfect, but doing so is not necessary.) Put a medium-sized cast-iron pan on medium-high heat and add a drizzle of melted butter, using a pastry brush to gloss the pan. Start layering the potato slices in a spiral design, overlapping each slice. Drizzle a bit of butter over the layer and sprinkle on a bit of salt and a grind of pepper. Repeat this process (still working with the pan on the stove), layering the potatoes, drizzling with butter and sprinkling with salt and pepper, pressing the potatoes down with a metal spatula as you work. By the time you have finished, it will be time to remove the pan from the heat. (If you are working very slowly, remove the pan from the heat before you have finished layering the potatoes.) Now, drizzle the last bit of butter over the surface. Using a large metal spatula, press down on the potato cake. Butter a circle of parchment paper and lay it on the top of the potatoes. Place a weight of some sort—half of a brick wrapped in foil is perfect—on top.

Bake for about 45 minutes, until the edges of the potato are golden brown and the centre is tender when pierced with a skewer. Remove the pan from the oven. Slide a thin spatula around the edge and give the pan a knock. Place a warmed, round serving plate on top of the skillet and quickly invert the cake onto the plate. (For a less formal presentation, just bring the skillet to the table.) Cut the potato cake into wedges and serve them upside down.

Spicy Matchsticks

2–3 cloves garlic, peeled

1–2 dried chiles

1 medium onion, roughly chopped

Vegetable oil

1 tsp (5 mL) cumin

1/2 tsp (2 mL) coriander

1 lb (500 g) baking potatoes, peeled

Salt

Place the garlic, chiles and onion in a blender or food processor. Pulse until a paste forms, adding a very little oil if necessary and scraping the sides of the bowl down with a rubber spatula. Scrape this mixture into a mixing bowl and add the cumin and coriander, blending in well with the spatula. Set the spice mixture aside.

Cut the potatoes into 1/8-inch (3 mm) slices (use a mandoline if you have one). Pile the slices into short stacks and then slice them into 1/8-inch (3 mm) wide sticks. Have ready a baking sheet lined with paper toweling. Heat some oil in a deep fryer or other heavy, deep pot to 375°F (190°C). If you are not using a deep-fryer, use a candy thermometer to gauge the temperature of the oil. Carefully place a portion of the potatoes in the hot oil without overcrowding them. Stir and fry the potato sticks until they are golden and beginning to crisp, turning them around with a slotted spoon. Remove them with the slotted spoon as they are done and drain them on the paper toweling. When all the potatoes are done, place about 4 tablespoons (60 mL) oil in a large, heavy frying pan. Add the reserved spice mixture and fry it in the oil over medium heat, stirring, until the mixture becomes quite aromatic and dry and begins to brown. Be very careful not to burn the spice mixture. After a few minutes, add the fried potatoes to the pan and use tongs to toss them in the spice mixture until they are well coated. Sprinkle with salt. Serve immediately in paper cones made of parchment paper.

Everybody knows that potatoes make great snacks in the form of chips, crisps and the like. And while you'd probably never dream of serving dinner guests their own little paper cone of potato chips (unless, of course, you had made them), you will certainly want to make these Indian-style potato sticks for just that purpose.

French Potato Galette

MAKES 1 SERVING

A real galette is a round, flat cake or sometimes a tart, savoury or sweet. In this recipe, the galette consists of a series of ultra-thin slices of potato that are set in a sort of a circle in a heavy skillet and fried on both sides until the potato slices are linked and the whole thing resembles one giant potato chip! You have to make galettes one at a time, so if you plan on making a few, keep them warm in a low oven, although I have to say they really are best just scarfed up as they are made. The finished galette can be served as a side dish on its own, or use it as a foundation for a thick piece of seared salmon or tuna.

1 large baking potato, peeled
1 tbsp (15 mL) butter, melted

1 tbsp (15 mL) extra virgin olive oil
Salt and freshly ground pepper

Slice the potatoes lengthwise very thinly, at least 1/8-inch (3 mm) thick, with a sharp chef's knife or on a mandoline. Combine the butter and oil in a medium-sized mixing bowl. Add the potato slices to the bowl and season with salt and pepper. Use your hands to make sure the potatoes are well coated with the butter, oil, salt and pepper. In a nonstick skillet or a well-seasoned cast-iron skillet, arrange a dozen of the largest slices of potato in a circle, slightly overlapping their edges. The circle should radiate from the centre of the skillet. Place the pan over medium-high heat for about 12 minutes, and then gently lift the edges of the potato slices with a metal spatula and give the pan a shake to free the galette from the bottom of the pan. At this point, the potato should be in one mass. Flip it over and cook the other side for about 6 minutes. Keep flipping once or twice more for a total of about 2 minutes until the potato is cooked through and beautifully golden brown and very crisp. Sprinkle with a little salt and a grind of pepper. Serve at once.

Paper Bag Potatoes

MAKES 4 TO 6 SERVINGS

24 small potatoes, scrubbed

3 tbsp (45 mL) chopped fresh mint

2 tbsp (30 mL) chopped fresh
   flat-leaf parsley

Salt and freshly ground pepper

4 tbsp (60 mL) butter, diced

Preheat the oven to 350°F (180°C). Arrange the potatoes on a piece of parchment paper laid over a baking sheet. Make sure the piece of parchment is large enough to enclose the potatoes. (You can also use foil.) Scatter the fresh herbs over the potatoes, season with salt and pepper and dot with the diced butter. Loosely enfold the potatoes in the parchment paper, being careful not to wrap the potatoes too tightly. Bake the package for about 45 minutes. Transfer to a serving plate and slit the package open at the table.

 While several thousand potato varieties exist throughout the world, only a fraction of them are actually in annual production. So many factors must be considered before a potato variety gains real popularity: resistance to disease, storage capabilities and whether a specific variety has the cooking characteristics that may currently be in demand for that type of potato.

This, of course, is cooking en papillote, a method whereby food is cooked in a parchment paper pouch. The idea is that the steam created in the parcel helps cook the food, the flavours are sealed in and, when the paper is slit open at the table, wonderfully fragrant aromas are released. This method is a great treatment for new small potatoes as their delightful flavour is kept intact. You can actually use a sturdy brown paper bag to prepare these aromatic little spuds, but I think parchment paper folded like a package is preferable. Paper bag potatoes are a lovely choice to serve with baby lamb and the first asparagus of the season.

White Purée Avalon

This is such an understated moniker for such an elegant side dish. Chef Chris McDonald of Toronto's Avalon restaurant features this satin-smooth root vegetable purée with his fabulous bone-in sirloins. While the original recipe included white turnip, I decided to pump up the potato content a bit. Either way, this dish is also wonderful with any number of rustic stew-like preparations.

1 medium celeriac, peeled, cubed

Salt

3 large floury potatoes, peeled, quartered

1 head garlic, cloves separated, peeled

1 large leek, white and pale green part only, chopped

1 medium onion, quartered

1 cup (250 mL) cooked white beans, drained

1/4 lb (125 g) unsalted butter

Place the celeriac in a large pot of boiling, salted water and cook for 15 minutes. Add the potatoes, garlic, leek and onion. Cook at a light boil until all the vegetables are tender, about 30 minutes. Drain the vegetables and return them to the pot.

Combine the beans with the vegetables. In portions, pass the mixture through a large, fine sieve using a wooden pestle or similar tool to push it through (alternatively, use a food mill—but not a food processor—to purée the vegetables). Wipe the pot clean and return the purée to it. Reheat the purée over medium heat, stirring rapidly and constantly with a wooden spoon to prevent sticking. Remove from the heat and add the butter, stirring until it is fully incorporated. Serve the purée at once.

Grand Luxe Gratin

MAKES 4 SERVINGS

5 tbsp (75 mL) butter

2 cloves garlic, halved

6 large baking potatoes, peeled,
   thinly sliced

Salt and freshly ground pepper

2 cups (500 mL) grated Gruyère cheese

3 eggs, beaten

2 cups (500 mL) heavy cream

Preheat the oven to 350°F (180°C). Use a little of the butter to lightly grease a 10-inch (25 cm) oval gratin dish. Rub the dish well with the garlic halves. Arrange a third of the sliced potatoes in the dish, dot with some of the butter and season with salt and pepper. Repeat the process with another layer of potatoes, but also scatter on a portion of the Gruyère cheese. Repeat with the remaining potatoes and butter. Transfer the gratin dish to a baking sheet covered with parchment paper or foil. Place the baking sheet holding the gratin dish on the middle rack of the oven. Combine the eggs and cream and carefully pour the mixture over the potatoes, making sure you just cover them. Distribute the remaining cheese over the surface of the potatoes. Bake for 1 hour and 15 minutes, or until the potatoes are cooked through and the top is golden brown and bubbly. (If the top browns too quickly, cover loosely with foil for the last bit of cooking time.) Remove from the oven and let sit for 5 minutes or so before serving.

If this gratin were a train, it would be the Orient Express. If it were a hotel, it would be New York's St. Regis. If it were a dress, it would be a ballgown by Valentino and if it were a single malt scotch, it would be a 32-year-old Ardbeg. Well, you get the picture. It's big, it's over the top and it's all yours to enjoy at least once a year. Buy a pound or so of assorted wild mushrooms, sauté with a few crushed garlic cloves in butter and then use the mixture as a centre layer in this gratin if you want to make your guests swoon.

Crispy Potato Nests with Scallops & Shrimp

MAKES 6 SERVINGS

The trick to this impressive little dish is readiness. A willing sidekick wouldn't hurt either. Read the recipe through and make sure you have everything at hand in the state required. You will need two long-handled wire strainers, one slightly smaller than the other, to prepare the potato nests. You place the raw potato mixture in the larger strainer and use the smaller strainer to press down on the potato mixture to form it into a cup shape. Holding the handles of both strainers tightly together, you then lower the strainers into the hot oil to cook the nest. The process is quite easy, really, and doesn't take long. These crispy little nests can hold barbecued pork and peppers, chicken and broccoli, chunks of fish or any number of stir-fry preparations. Keep the baskets hot in a warm oven while you prepare the filling.

FOR THE FILLING:

1 lb (500 g) large shrimp, shelled, deveined, halved

2 tbsp (30 mL) lemon juice

1 lb (500 g) large scallops, halved

2 tbsp (30 mL) milk

3 tbsp (45 mL) vegetable oil

1 tsp (5 mL) sesame oil

1/2 lb (250 g) snowpeas

2 tbsp (30 mL) hoisin sauce

FOR THE POTATO NESTS:

6 large baking potatoes, peeled, coarsely grated

2 tbsp (30 mL) cornstarch

Vegetable oil

Combine the shrimp and the lemon juice in a bowl. In another bowl, combine the scallops with the milk. Set both mixtures to one side.

Next, prepare the potato nests. Warm the oven. Place the grated potato in a clean tea towel and squeeze it over the sink to remove any trace of moisture. Pat the potato dry with another tea towel if necessary. Combine the potato with the cornstarch in a bowl. Brush a little oil on each of the strainers. Heat some oil in a deep-fryer or other heavy, deep pot to 350°F (180°C). If you are not using a deep-fryer, use a candy thermometer to gauge the temperature of the oil. Place one-sixth of the potato mixture in the larger of the two strainers. Now, press the smaller strainer on top, pressing the potato down to form a cup shape. Holding the handles of both strainers firmly together, lower the strainers into the hot oil and cook until the potato nest is crispy and golden brown, just a few minutes. Carefully remove the potato nest from the strainer by tapping the nest out onto paper towel–lined baking sheet. Repeat with the remaining potato mixture, keeping the cooked nests warm in a low oven.

To finish preparing the filling, drain the shrimp and scallops (discard the liquids). Heat the vegetable oil and sesame oil in a wok or sauté pan, add the shrimp and scallops and stir-fry for 2 minutes. Add the snowpeas and the hoisin sauce and stir-fry for another minute, or until the shrimp and scallops are just cooked. Place the potato baskets on a serving plate, fill the baskets with the seafood mixture and serve immediately.

 By the end of the 18th century, the potato was an important crop in Europe, particularly in Germany, England and, of course, Ireland. At that time, poor Irish families ate a daily average of 10 potatoes per person. The potato constituted 80 percent of their diet, which made the potato blight that struck in the 1840s all the more disastrous. The Irish are credited with popularizing the potato in North America, to which they moved in great numbers because of the famine in Ireland. Consequently, the white potato became known in North America as the Irish or Murphy's potato.

Onion & Potato Cake

MAKES 6 SERVINGS

Here is a simple yet satisfying potato cake that is based on mashed potato. Nice for breakfast, brunch or as part of a light supper, this dish is particularly good for serving to company as it can be made ahead up to the point at which you brown and crisp it under a broiler. This potato cake is a great accompaniment to marinated flank steak or pork tenderloin.

5 large floury potatoes, peeled	3 large onions, thinly sliced
Salt	1 cup (250 mL) grated Emmental cheese
1/4 cup + 2 tbsp (60 + 30 mL) butter	Salt and freshly ground pepper

Place the potatoes in a large saucepan, cover them with cold water and bring to a boil. Add a little salt, reduce the heat and cook for 25 to 30 minutes until the potatoes are soft. Drain thoroughly, return the potatoes to low heat and shake the pan to remove any trace of moisture. Mash the potatoes roughly with a large fork.

Heat the 1/4 cup (60 mL) butter over medium heat in a heavy, ovenproof skillet. Add the onions and sauté until they are soft and lightly browned. Add the onions to the potatoes in the saucepan, along with the cheese, salt and pepper and blend well. In the same skillet, melt the remaining 2 tablespoons (30 mL) butter, add the potato mixture and press down firmly with a metal spatula. Cover the skillet and cook the potato mixture over moderate heat until the bottom of the cake is browned. Meanwhile, preheat the oven broiler. When it is hot, place the skillet in the oven about 5 to 6 inches (12–15 cm) below the broiler and broil until the potato cake is crisp and brown. Remove it from the oven and let stand for 10 minutes before serving.

Smoked Salmon Scalloped Spuds

MAKES 6 TO 8 SERVINGS

2 tbsp (30 mL) butter

8 red-skinned potatoes, cooked,
    peeled, sliced

1/2 lb (250 g) smoked salmon, cut into strips

6 green onions, finely chopped

3 cloves garlic, minced

Salt and freshly ground pepper

1 cup (250 mL) table cream

1/2 cup (125 mL) freshly grated
    Parmesan cheese

Preheat the oven to 350°F (180°C). Grease a baking dish with the butter. Add a layer of potatoes topped with a portion of salmon, onions, garlic and a little salt and pepper. Repeat the process with the remaining potatoes, salmon, garlic and all but a handful of the chopped green onion.

Transfer the dish to a baking sheet covered with parchment paper. Place the baking sheet holding the dish on the middle rack of the oven. Carefully pour the cream over the potatoes. Scatter the cheese over the surface and bake for 45 minutes, or until golden brown and crispy. Remove the potatoes from the oven and let stand for 10 minutes or so before serving sprinkled with the reserved green onions.

When you are planning a Sunday brunch gathering, put this dish together the night before. Let the dish sit at room temperature for a while before baking in the oven. Serve these scalloped potatoes with scrambled eggs with chives and pan-seared tomato halves. You can make this preparation with uncooked potatoes, too; just increase the oven time by about 20 minutes and add an extra 1/2 cup (125 mL) cream or milk.

Fulton Fish Market Chowder

MAKES 6 SERVINGS

In homage to New York City's fabulous Fulton Fish Market, where there are hundreds of species of fish from which to choose, this Manhattan-style fish and potato soup is ultra-easy and quick to put together. So, organize a kitchen party, pour everyone a glass of wine and get to it! Serve this delicious chowder with lots of good, buttered bread.

6 strips unsmoked bacon, diced
2 cloves garlic, crushed
1 large white onion, chopped
1 yellow or orange bell pepper, seeded, thinly sliced
2 tbsp (30 mL) chopped fresh flat-leaf parsley
1 can (28 oz/796 mL) plum tomatoes
2 1/2 cups (625 mL) clam juice
1 cup (250 mL) light red wine

1 tbsp (15 mL) chopped fresh thyme
Salt and freshly ground pepper
3 large waxy, red-skinned potatoes, scrubbed, cut into small chunks
1/2 lb (250 g) salmon fillet, cut into small chunks
1/2 lb (250 g) scallops
1 lb (500 g) small shrimp, shelled, deveined
1/2 cup (125 mL) chopped fresh cilantro

In a large, heavy-based soup pot or Dutch oven, sauté the bacon until it is crisp; don't drain. Add the garlic, onion, bell pepper and parsley and sauté over medium heat for 10 minutes or so, stirring frequently. Add the tomatoes and their juice, breaking the tomatoes up roughly in the pot. Add the clam juice, red wine and thyme and season with salt and pepper. Give the mixture a good stir and bring it to a boil. Reduce the heat and simmer for 15 or 20 minutes. Add the potatoes and cook for another 15 minutes, or until the potatoes are tender. Add the salmon, making sure it is submerged in the soup. Cook for 5 minutes, add the scallops and shrimp and cook for another 5 minutes. Ladle the chowder into bowls, sprinkle with the cilantro and serve.

Baby Potatoes
with Salsa Verde

FOR THE SALSA VERDE:

1 bunch fresh flat-leaf parsley, rinsed, dried

12 fresh basil leaves

4 anchovy fillets

2 tbsp (30 mL) capers, drained

2 cloves garlic, roughly chopped

6–8 pitted green olives, roughly chopped

1 tbsp (15 mL) malt vinegar

1 thick slice bread, crusts removed, torn
   into pieces

1 cup (250 mL) extra virgin olive oil

Salt and freshly ground pepper

FOR THE POTATOES:

30 baby potatoes, washed, cooked as
   you prefer

Remove the leaves from the parsley stems. Place the parsley leaves in a food processor along with the basil, anchovy fillets, capers, garlic, olives, vinegar and bread. Pulse the mixture, scraping the sides of the processor bowl down from time to time. Now, with the processor running, add the olive oil in a gradual stream. When the oil is thoroughly incorporated, turn off the processor and season the mixture with salt and pepper. Scrape the salsa into a serving bowl and serve with the hot potatoes. If you are using this preparation as a side dish, drizzle a little salsa verde over each serving and pass the remainder at the table.

Watch these babies disappear at your next soirée. Choose the smallest new potatoes you can find for this little dish, which can be served as hors d'oeuvres or a side dish. Depending on the time of year, you may choose to steam, boil, bake or grill the potatoes before serving them with this, the ultimate in piquant green sauces. If you plan to grill them, precook the potatoes for a few minutes on high in your microwave.

Short Ribs of Beef with Soaked Spuds

Short ribs of beef make one of the most satisfying of dishes, slowly cooked so that the meat is fork-tender. In this dish of old-fashioned flavours, halves of potatoes form the bed for the beef and soak up the lovely, rich essence of the meat as it cooks. Make the preparations for this dish the night before.

MAKES 4 SERVINGS

3 lbs (1.5 kg) beef short ribs, 2-inches (5 cm) thick

6 slices bacon, chopped

2 large onions, quartered

1 bottle (750 mL) dry white wine

1 tsp (5 mL) salt

1 tsp (5 mL) freshly ground pepper

6 sprigs fresh flat-leaf parsley

2 sprigs fresh rosemary

2 sprigs fresh thyme

1 bay leaf

1 small leek, split, rinsed, halved

2 tbsp (30 mL) butter

2 tbsp (30 mL) all-purpose flour

2 lbs (1 kg) medium red-skinned potatoes, scrubbed, halved

1/4 cup (60 mL) chopped fresh flat-leaf parsley

Ask the butcher to keep the short ribs in pairs and cut them 2-inches (5 cm) thick. Before you marinate them, trim as much of the fat from the ribs as possible; otherwise your sauce will be too fatty. Place the ribs in a large bowl and add the bacon, onions, wine, salt and pepper. Make a bouquet garni by tying together the parsley, rosemary, thyme, bay leaf and leek. Put the bouquet garni well down amid the ribs. Using your hands, mix the ingredients well. Cover and refrigerate overnight.

Preheat the oven to 350°F (180°C). Remove the ribs from the marinade (reserve it) and, using a slotted spoon, retrieve the bits of bacon. Melt the butter in a large, heavy roasting pan or Dutch oven (either must have a lid) and sauté the bacon and ribs, turning once or twice, for about 12 minutes, until the beef is lightly browned on all sides. Using tongs, remove the onion pieces and the bouquet garni from the marinade, and add them to the roasting pan and cook for another 12 minutes. Sprinkle the ingredients with the flour, toss to combine well and cook for another 5 minutes, stirring to dissolve and cook the flour. Now, add the potatoes, pushing them down around the meat. Pour the reserved marinade over the ingredients and add a bit more salt and pepper. Mix again, cover and bake for 2 hours, longer if the meat and potatoes were thickly cut. Stir the mixture frequently as it bakes. When the meat and potatoes are tender, remove from the oven. Discard the bouquet garni, sprinkle with the chopped parsley and serve.

The potato is one of the highest sources of vitamin C of any vegetable in the North American diet and contains only a trace of fat and very little sodium. A medium spud contains a little over 200 calories and is also an excellent source of vitamin B_6 and niacin and a good source of potassium and fibre.

Oyster Pie with Top Mash

Now, here's one for Christmas Eve or maybe New Year's Eve. Choose this fabulous pie when you are feeling flush with moolah, when you've just received a long-awaited raise, when you've finally lost the last five pounds or when none of the above apply but you want to feel as though they did. If it is possible for something to be at once elegant and comforting, this dish—which brings Ireland to mind—is it. Buy fresh oysters from a reputable supplier and explain how you will be using them. Good suppliers know their stuff and will recommend the best oysters for the job and be happy to shuck them for you. Ask the fishmonger to give you the liquor from the oysters. Oysters for this dish should be firm and slightly salty, like bluepoints from the Atlantic or Quilcene oysters from Puget Sound. Make the mashed potato topping first and keep it warm.

MAKES 4 TO 6 SERVINGS

FOR THE POTATOES:

2 lbs (1 kg) floury potatoes, peeled, quartered

1 tsp (5 mL) salt

1/2 cup (125 mL) butter

3/4 cup (150 mL) whole milk or buttermilk (approx.)

1/2 cup (125 mL) table cream

1/2 cup (125 mL) finely chopped fresh chives

FOR THE OYSTERS:

4 slices bacon, diced

1 white onion, chopped

1 carrot, scraped, grated

1 small red bell pepper, seeded, finely chopped

1 cup (250 mL) corn kernels, fresh or frozen; if frozen, thawed, drained

1 cup (250 mL) peas, fresh or frozen; if frozen, thawed, drained

24 oysters, shucked, liquor reserved

Chicken broth, as needed

6 tbsp (90 mL) butter

6 tbsp (90 mL) all-purpose flour

1 cup (250 mL) heavy cream

Salt and freshly ground pepper

Preheat the oven to 400°F (200°C). Place the potatoes in a medium-sized saucepan, cover with cold water, bring to a boil over high heat and add the salt. Reduce the heat slightly and boil until the potatoes are tender right through, about 20 minutes. Remove from the heat and drain the potatoes, keeping them in the saucepan. Return the saucepan to the heat, reduced to as low as possible. Shake the saucepan on the heat a few times, until all traces of moisture have evaporated. Add the butter and mash it into the potatoes well. Gradually add the milk or buttermilk and the table cream, mashing the potatoes well after each addition. Using a flat whisk or wooden spoon, stir rapidly to incorporate a little air into the mash. When it is smooth and creamy, fold in the chopped chives. Cover the mashed potatoes with a clean tea towel and the saucepan lid. Keep warm.

Sauté the bacon over medium heat in a large skillet until almost cooked. Drain off half the fat. Add the onion to the bacon and sauté a few minutes until softened. Add the carrot, sauté for a couple of minutes and then add the bell pepper, corn and peas, continuing to cook for about 3 minutes. As the mixture cooks, pour the reserved oyster liquor into a 2-cup (500 mL) measuring cup and add enough chicken broth to fill it. Reserve.

Add the butter to the vegetables, allow it to melt and then add the flour, using a flat whisk to incorporate the flour into the butter. Allow the flour to cook for a few minutes. Then, slowly add the oyster liquor and chicken broth combination, still whisking to prevent the mixture from lumping. Cook for a few minutes longer, continuing to stir, and then gradually add the heavy cream, stirring continually. Season with salt and pepper and cook at a gentle simmer for about 5 minutes, until the mixture is thick and smooth.

Using a sharp knife, cut the oysters in half (do this on a board with grooves so as not to lose any residual liquor). Remove the pan from the heat and gently stir the oysters into the sauce. Pour the mixture into a gratin dish or shallow baking dish. Pile the mashed potatoes on top of the oyster filling, using a wide metal spatula to dab the mash into place, allowing it to rise in peaks here and there. (If you like, you can use a piping bag to pipe the potato mixture over the oyster filling.) Bake the oyster pie for about 20 minutes, until the filling is bubbling round the edges and the potatoes are golden brown with crisp peaks. Let sit for 5 minutes before serving.

Hot Szechwan Salt
& Pepper Potatoes

MAKES 4 SERVINGS

You can hardly get more basic than potatoes and salt, but when the "salt" in question is a combination of kosher salt, dried chiles, a little five-spice powder and Szechwan peppercorns, it's a whole different ballgame. You have to parboil (or microwave) the potatoes for this dish; if you like, do so ahead of time, even the day before, and then fry the potatoes just before serving. This seasoning recipe will make a lot more of the spicy salt than you will need for one recipe, so store the rest in a clean jar with a tight-fitting lid. It's a great spice mixture to have on hand for many things—try it rubbed into shrimp before a quick grilling. Look for Szechwan peppercorns in Asian supermarkets or specialty food shops.

FOR THE SZECHWAN SALT AND PEPPER:

2–4 whole dried chiles

1/2 cup (125 mL) salt

1/4 cup (60 mL) Szechwan peppercorns

1 tbsp (15 mL) coriander seeds

1 tbsp (15 mL) cumin seeds

1 tbsp (15 mL) fennel seeds

1 tsp (5 mL) Chinese five-spice powder

FOR THE POTATOES:

2 lbs (1 kg) small, new potatoes, rinsed, halved

1 tsp (5 mL) salt

Vegetable oil as needed

1/2–1 tsp (2–5 mL) Szechwan salt and pepper

1/2 cup (125 mL) chopped fresh cilantro

Make the Szechwan salt and pepper first. Grind the chiles in a coffee mill and place them in a bowl with the salt. Then combine the remaining ingredients in the coffee mill, grind to a powder and add to the ground chiles and salt. Mix well.

Place the potatoes in a large saucepan, cover them with boiling water, add the salt and bring back to a boil. Reduce the heat and cook for about 3 to 4 minutes; don't cook the potatoes all the way through. Drain and let cool.

Heat about 2 inches (5 cm) oil in a deep-fryer or other deep, heavy pot to 375°F (190°C). If you are not using a deep-fryer, use a candy thermometer to gauge the temperature of the oil. Make sure the potatoes are completely dry, and then add one-third of them to the oil. Fry for just under 2 minutes; if the potatoes are very small, 1 1/2 minutes should do it. Use a slotted spoon or wire mesh strainer to remove the potatoes from the oil. Drain them on paper toweling. Let the oil return to the cooking temperature and repeat the process twice with the remaining potatoes. Transfer the cooked potatoes to a large mixing bowl and toss them with the Szechwan salt and pepper and the fresh cilantro. Serve immediately.

Cantal & Potato Purée with Parsley Garlic Butter

FOR THE GARLIC BUTTER:

1/4 lb (125 g) butter

2 cloves garlic, crushed

4 tbsp (60 mL) chopped fresh
   flat-leaf parsley

1/4 tsp (1 mL) Dijon mustard

2 tbsp (30 mL) lemon juice

Salt and freshly ground pepper

FOR THE POTATO PURÉE:

2 lb (1 kg) floury potatoes, peeled, quartered

Salt

4 strips bacon, diced

3/4 cup (175 mL) whole milk

4 tbsp (60 mL) butter

1 lb (500 g) Cantal cheese, slivered

You know the lovely, buttery mixture that French bistros reserve for escargot? Well, here it is licking up the sides of a sumptuous mash of potatoes and Cantal, the rich, nutty Cheddar-like cheese from France. Have your loving kitchen partner quickly sear a few flattened, boneless chicken breasts or scallops to serve atop this mixture (it's very good with sausages, too) as you prepare the purée. Easy and quite delicious.

To prepare the garlic butter, melt the butter over low heat in a small saucepan. Add the garlic, increase heat slightly and sauté the garlic, but do not let it brown. Gently stir in the parsley and mustard. Remove the pan from the heat and, when cool, whisk in the lemon juice and season with a little salt and pepper. Set to one side.

Place the potatoes in a large saucepan, cover them with cold water and bring to a boil. Add a little salt and boil gently until the potatoes are cooked, about 20 minutes. As the potatoes cook, fry the bacon until it is crisp. Set to one side. Drain the potatoes and dry them thoroughly, shaking them in the saucepan over low heat a few times. Mash the potatoes well, adding the milk and butter as you make a smooth purée. Fold in the cooked bacon and place the saucepan over quite low heat. Fold in the slivered cheese gradually, beating well after each addition. When all the cheese has been incorporated, gently reheat the parsley garlic butter. Drizzle it over the purée and serve.

Potato Soup with Pesto

MAKES 4 TO 6 SERVINGS

This luxurious, silky smooth potato soup showcases a brilliant emerald mound of pesto floating on the surface—perfect for St. Patrick's Day dinners. Make the pesto ahead of time. If you can't obtain enough fresh basil, look for a good quality jarred pesto for this recipe. Crème fraîche is often available at a good cheesemonger or in some specialty food shops. You can easily make your own, though. See page 40. Serve this soup with thin slices of toasted baguette.

FOR THE PESTO:

1 large clove garlic

1/2 tsp (2 mL) salt

2 cups (250 mL) lightly packed fresh basil leaves

1/2 cup (125 mL) extra virgin olive oil

1 1/2 tbsp (20 mL) pine nuts or walnuts

1/2 cup (125 mL) grated Pecorino Romano cheese

1 cup crème fraîche

Salt and freshly ground pepper

FOR THE SOUP:

1/4 cup (60 mL) butter

4 cloves garlic, peeled, crushed

1 bay leaf

1 sprig fresh thyme

1 medium leek (white part only), rinsed, chopped

1 small onion, chopped

1 stalk celery, trimmed, chopped

3 large floury potatoes, peeled, sliced

1 1/2 cups (375 mL) chicken broth

1 1/2 cups (375 mL) heavy cream

3 tbsp (45 mL) buttermilk

Salt and freshly ground pepper

First, make the pesto: crush the garlic with the salt and place the mixture in a blender or food processor along with the basil, olive oil and nuts. Blend until the ingredients are finely puréed. Using a rubber spatula, scrape the basil mixture into a small mixing bowl. Fold in the grated cheese and blend well. Carefully stir in the crème fraîche. Season with salt and pepper. Cover and refrigerate until ready to use.

Now, make the soup: melt the butter in a large saucepan over medium heat. Add the garlic, bay leaf, thyme, leek, onion and celery and cook gently, reducing the heat after a minute or two, until the vegetables are quite tender, about 5 minutes. Do not allow them to brown at all. Add the potatoes, chicken broth and cream. If the potatoes aren't totally submerged in the liquid, add a little water. Simmer the mixture for about 20 minutes, or until the potatoes are cooked through and tender. Purée the potato mixture using a hand-held blender or a blender or food processor. Stir in the buttermilk. Wipe the saucepan clean and pour the puréed soup through a fine sieve back into the saucepan. Season with salt and pepper. Ladle the soup while it is still very hot into soup bowls and place a good dollop of pesto in the centre of each serving. Run a toothpick through the pesto to drag it out decoratively over the surface of the soup.

 In Europe it is more common for potato growers, marketers and buyers to identify potatoes by their variety name, whereas in North America most wholesalers dub the spud with a moniker that relates to the location where the potato was grown—hence Idaho and P.E.I. potatoes. However, the famed Canadian potato known as the Yukon Gold has nothing to do with the Yukon. The variety's developer, the late Garnett Johnston, chose the name in reference to the potato's gold flesh and the legendary Yukon gold rush.

Pork Steaks with Dijon Cream & Pomme Fondant

Pomme fondant is the classic name for big, thick ovals or circles of potato fried in butter until golden brown all over and cooked through. They benefit by being made about an hour ahead so they can absorb the butter. Fresh, boneless pork steaks are available from quality butchers and, I think, are as satisfying as a good beef strip loin. However, beef, pork, lamb chops or even boneless chicken breasts can be used here as the smooth mustard sauce goes very well with many meats. Serve with sautéed rapini or a crisp green salad that contains some bitter greens.

FOR THE POTATOES:
6 medium Yukon Gold potatoes, peeled
6 tbsp (90 mL) unsalted butter, diced
Salt and freshly ground pepper
1/4 cup (60 mL) water

FOR THE MEAT:
6 boneless pork steaks,
   1 1/4-inch (3 cm) thick

1/4 cup (60 mL) olive oil
Salt and freshly ground black pepper
2/3 cup (150 mL) cognac or brandy
1 1/2 cups (375 mL) beef broth
2–3 tbsp (30–45 mL) cold butter
1/3 cup (75 mL) heavy cream
3 tbsp (45 mL) Dijon mustard
1/2 cup (125 mL) chopped fresh
   flat-leaf parsley

Square off each potato by slicing a bit from each end and each side. Using a 2-inch (5 cm) biscuit cutter, cut through each potato to achieve a cylindrical shape. You can use this shape or go for the classic oval shape by further trimming the potato's edges to achieve a shape like a large olive. (Save the potato bits for another use.) Place the diced butter in a saucepan or skillet large enough to hold all the carved potato pieces in one layer without crowding. Place the potatoes in the pan and season with salt and pepper. Place the pan over medium heat and, as the butter melts, add the water and cook the potatoes on low heat for about 15 to 20 minutes, until they are golden brown on both sides, turning them a few times to achieve this. As the potatoes cook, add a little more butter or water if the pan is about to dry out totally. When the potatoes are cooked through, set them to one side and keep warm as you make the pork steaks.

Pat the steaks dry with paper toweling. Rub the surfaces of the steaks with the oil, rubbing it in well. Sprinkle the meat generously with salt and pepper. Place a heavy frying pan or skillet over medium-high heat and allow it to get quite hot.

Sear the steaks for about 5 seconds on each side. Reduce the heat to medium and cook the steaks to your taste (about 4 minutes on each side for medium). Transfer them to a warm platter.

Splash the cognac or brandy into the hot pan, scraping the bottom of the pan to loosen any bits of meat. Cook for 1 minute to evaporate the alcohol; add the beef broth. Continue to cook on relatively high heat to reduce the liquid by one-third. Reduce the heat to medium.

Add the butter in pieces and stir to blend it into the sauce. Whisk the cream and mustard into the sauce and continue to cook until all ingredients are well blended and the sauce has thickened.

Pour the sauce over the steaks and sprinkle with chopped parsley. Serve immediately with the pomme fondant.

 Winston Churchill described fish and chips—arguably England's national dish—as "the good companions," not only because of their seemingly natural compatibility, but also because, from the late 19th century on, they provided deliciously good nutrition for the hungry working class at a comparatively low cost.

Potatoes in the summer lend their particular magic to so many dishes, mostly because so much food is available at this bountiful time of the year. Ripe tomatoes, fresh corn, baby lettuces and other greens and all the traditional grill items—each of these components lends inspiration to those of us who look for potatoes on their plate every day. You would expect this section of the book to be filled with potato salads, and that is just as it should be. So many wonderful variations—from classics to contemporary renditions and everything in between—can be enjoyed during the hot summer months. This is the time of year when lovely little new potatoes are available, as well as many other varieties that are not always in wide supply. So, while you'll find endless inspiration here salad-wise, you'll also find recipes for other types of preparations.

the
summer potato

Grilled Red Potato Salad with Basil Aïoli

MAKES 4 TO 6 SERVINGS

What would food from the south of France be without aïoli, that region's characteristically pungent garlic sauce that is so ubiquitous it is known as beurre de Provence? Aïoli is wonderful with any grilled vegetables or seafood but is especially memorable with new potatoes. Although the basil is not a traditional ingredient, it makes a lovely difference. Use waxy red- or white-skinned potatoes. Wooden skewers (soaked beforehand) work best because the potatoes won't slip around as they often do on metal skewers.

FOR THE AÏOLI:
4 cloves garlic, minced
2 large egg yolks
2 tbsp (30 mL) fresh lemon juice
1/2 tsp (2 mL) coarse salt
1/4 tsp (1 mL) freshly ground pepper
3/4 cup (175 mL) extra virgin olive oil
1/2 cup (125 mL) chopped fresh basil

FOR THE POTATOES:
1 lb (500 kg) new potatoes, scrubbed
1/4 cup (60 mL) extra virgin olive oil
1 tbsp (15 mL) dried basil
Salt and freshly ground pepper

First, prepare the aïoli. Combine the garlic, egg yolks, lemon juice, salt and pepper in a blender or food processor. Pulse on and off a few times until blended. With the motor running, gradually drizzle in the olive oil. Continue to blend until the mixture becomes creamy and thick.

Transfer the mixture to a bowl and fold in the basil. Cover and refrigerate until 30 minutes before ready to use. Preheat the grill.

Place the potatoes in a bowl and add the olive oil, basil and salt and pepper. Toss together to coat the potatoes thoroughly. Thread them onto skewers and grill over medium heat until the skins begin to brown and crisp, about 25 to 30 minutes, turning the skewers frequently. (You can speed things up a bit by precooking pierced potatoes for about 5 minutes on high in the microwave prior to grilling.) When the potatoes are cooked through, transfer them to a serving platter. Pour the aïoli into an attractive serving jug and serve alongside the potatoes.

Fingerling Potatoes with Tarragon Cream

MAKES 6 TO 8 SERVINGS

2 lbs (1 kg) fingerling potatoes,
  scrubbed, halved

Salt

1 shallot, peeled, minced

3 tbsp (45 mL) chopped fresh tarragon

3 tbsp (45 mL) white wine vinegar

Salt and freshly ground pepper

3 tbsp (45 mL) good quality mayonnaise

2 tbsp (30 mL) heavy cream

Place the potatoes in a saucepan, cover them with boiling water, add a little salt and bring to a boil. Cook for 15 minutes, or until the potatoes are tender. Drain and transfer them to a serving bowl. Add the shallot, tarragon, vinegar, salt and pepper. Toss together gently, then let cool slightly. Add the mayonnaise and cream and toss gently to coat the potatoes. Serve immediately.

I think the secret to the success of this delightful summer dish is to serve it just warm or as soon as it's ready. If left to cool, these lovely little waxy potatoes lose their characteristic interior stickiness, arguably one of their nicest features. Serve with cold ham, ripe tomatoes tossed with good olive oil and Boston lettuce.

Lobster & Potato Supper Salad

MAKES 6 SERVINGS

This salad is a good choice during June when fresh lobsters are a little more plentiful and priced somewhat more reasonably than at other times of the year. Having said that, either fresh, frozen or canned lobster may be used here.

3 green onions, trimmed, chopped

4 cups (1 L) cooked, diced new potatoes

2 cups (500 mL) cooked lobster, roughly chopped

1/2 lb (250 g) snowpeas, thinly sliced on an angle

Salt and freshly ground pepper

2/3 cup (150 mL) good quality mayonnaise

Juice of 1 small lemon

1/2 cup (125 mL) chopped fresh dill

1 head red oak-leaf lettuce, separated, rinsed, dried

Place the onions, potatoes, lobster and snowpeas in a large mixing bowl. Season with salt and pepper and toss the ingredients together. In a measuring cup, combine the mayonnaise with the lemon juice, whisking together with a fork. Pour the mayonnaise mixture over the lobster mixture, tossing well. Add the dill and toss again to combine. Cover with plastic wrap and refrigerate for about 1 hour. Arrange the leaf lettuce on plates, top with the lobster salad and serve.

Classic Salade Niçoise

MAKES 4 SERVINGS

FOR THE VINAIGRETTE:

1/4 cup (60 mL) extra virgin olive oil

1/4 cup (60 mL) vegetable oil
   (canola or sunflower)

2 tbsp (30 mL) white wine vinegar

2 tsp (10 mL) salt

1 tsp (5 mL) Dijon mustard

1 tsp (5 mL) freshly ground pepper

1 tsp (5 mL) lemon juice

1/2 tsp (2 mL) dry mustard

1/4 tsp (1 mL) sugar

FOR THE SALAD:

1 head Boston lettuce, rinsed, dried

2 1/2 cups (625 mL) diced cooked
   baking potatoes

2 cups (500 mL) cooked green
   beans, halved

1 1/2 cups (375 mL) drained canned white
   tuna, broken into chunks (approx. 3 cans)

3 medium tomatoes

4 hard-boiled eggs, quartered

8 anchovy fillets, drained on paper toweling

3/4 cup (175 mL) pitted black olives

1/4 cup (60 mL) chopped fresh
   flat-leaf parsley

This salad is often made these days using fresh tuna as many chefs strive to give this dish a modern appeal. While there is something to be said for creativity, I think the original version, based on good quality canned tuna, stands tallest and is the most summer friendly. You can use small new potatoes if you wish, but traditionally older potatoes are used, the better to soak up the great vinaigrette. Choose good quality, oil-packed tuna—not flaked. If you are not wild about anchovy, you may omit it. Serve with warmed baguette and a well-chilled Moselle.

First, place all the vinaigrette ingredients in a large jar and shake thoroughly. Set the vinaigrette to one side.

Wrap the lettuce leaves in paper toweling, place in a plastic bag and refrigerate while making the salad. Combine the potatoes, green beans and tuna in a large mixing bowl. Pour the vinaigrette over the tuna mixture, mix very lightly and allow the mixture to marinate about 1 hour, covered with a clean tea towel. (If the kitchen is very warm, refrigerate.) Using a vegetable peeler, peel the tomatoes and cut them into quarters. When ready to serve, line a shallow salad or pasta serving bowl with the lettuce leaves. Arrange the tuna mixture over the leaves. Place the tomato slices on and around the salad, along with the quartered eggs. If using the anchovy, lay half a fillet over each egg quarter. Scatter the olives and parsley over the salad and serve.

Baby Yukon Golds with Parsley & Crème Fraîche

MAKES 6 TO 8 SERVINGS

Any new potatoes can be used in this sweet little preparation. You can also vary the fresh herbs, using chives, chervil or basil as you wish. If you can find ready-made crème fraîche, by all means use it, or make your own a day before you make the salad.

FOR THE CRÈME FRAÎCHE (DAY AHEAD):
1 cup (250 mL) heavy cream
2 tbsp (30 mL) buttermilk or sour cream

FOR THE SALAD:
1 1/2 lbs (750 g) new Yukon Gold potatoes, scrubbed

Salt
3/4 cup (175 mL) heavy cream
2 shallots, peeled, finely diced
Salt and freshly ground pepper
1/2 cup (125 mL) crème fraîche
Splash of white wine vinegar
1/2 cup (125 mL) chopped fresh flat-leaf parsley

In a small saucepan, gently warm the heavy cream. Remove from the heat and combine with the buttermilk or sour cream in a glass bowl. Mix well, cover and let stand at room temperature overnight. Give the mixture a good stir once it has thickened. Cover and refrigerate. The crème fraîche will thicken even more once chilled.

Place the potatoes in a large saucepan, cover them with boiling water and add a little salt. Bring to a boil, reduce the heat and cook until the potatoes are tender, about 20 minutes. Drain and let cool.

At this point, if the potato skins are easy to pull off, do so; otherwise, just slice the potatoes into 1/4-inch (5 mm) slices.

Pour the heavy cream into a saucepan, add the shallots, season with salt and pepper and very gently warm the mixture over low heat. After a few minutes, when the shallots have softened, remove from heat and stir in the crème fraîche. Add the potatoes to the cream mixture, carefully stir to coat the potatoes, add a splash or two of vinegar, stir and let the mixture warm over low heat for just a minute. Add the chopped parsley, stir once more and serve immediately.

Rustic Summer Reds with Garlic & Fresh Herbs

MAKES 4 TO 6 SERVINGS

2 lbs (1 kg) large red-skinned
   potatoes, scrubbed

4 cloves garlic, minced

1/4 cup (60 mL) chopped fresh chives

1/4 cup (60 mL) chopped fresh mint

1/4 cup (60 mL) extra virgin olive oil

3 tbsp (45 mL) balsamic vinegar

Salt and freshly ground pepper

Cook the potatoes as you wish, but keep them whole. When they are just cool enough to handle, cut the potatoes into bite-sized chunks. In a large mixing bowl, mix the potatoes well with the garlic, chives, mint, oil, vinegar and salt and pepper. Before serving, let stand for 30 minutes or so at room temperature to allow the flavours to develop.

You might say that this is our "house" potato salad. My daughters and I make it often—during the summer and at other times of the year—when we want a big, garlicky hit of spuds and herbs. It's not delicate, but it is very good and also quite versatile as far as the cooking of the potatoes goes—either steam, boil, bake or grill them. Just make sure to combine the other in-gredients with the potatoes while they are still quite hot. These potatoes are great with grilled sausages and hot mustard.

Grilled Potato Wedges with Smoky Tomato & Chiles

MAKES 4 TO 6 SERVINGS

When your in-house grill master is bent on enjoying some really great homemade chips or oven fries to accompany the porterhouse steak he is masterfully grilling, tell him that it's too hot to heat up the kitchen and that these grilled spud wedges are the way to go. Even the ingredients for the accompanying chili sauce can be grilled, making this the perfect summer preparation. Get fired up and prepare the chili sauce first. It has a nice bit of heat and is outstanding with shrimp.

FOR THE CHILI SAUCE:

6 large ripe plum tomatoes

4 cloves garlic, unpeeled

3 fresh hot red chiles

1 medium onion, unpeeled, halved

1 small red bell pepper

3 tbsp (45 mL) extra virgin olive oil

3 tbsp (45 mL) finely chopped fresh cilantro

2 tsp (10 mL) brown sugar

2 tsp (10 mL) tomato paste

Juice of 1 lime

Salt and freshly ground pepper

FOR THE POTATOES:

6 large floury potatoes, scrubbed

2–3 tbsp (30–45 mL) olive oil

2 tsp (10 mL) paprika

Salt and freshly ground pepper

Prepare the ingredients for the sauce first. Preheat the grill to medium-high. Place the tomatoes, garlic, chiles, onion and bell pepper on a lightly greased grill (thread the garlic on presoaked wooden skewers or grill an entire head of garlic and keep some for another use). Grill the vegetables, turning them frequently, until they are charred and softened, transferring them as they are ready to a baking sheet. Let the vegetables cool slightly. Squeeze the garlic from its skin and peel off the onion skin. Don't bother to peel the tomatoes, chiles or bell pepper.

Place the vegetables in a food processor or blender. Add the olive oil, cilantro, sugar, tomato paste and lime juice to the vegetables and process until blended to a thick sauce. Season with a little salt and pepper. Set to one side to allow the flavours to develop while you prepare the potatoes.

Preheat the grill. Slice the potatoes into thick wedges. Toss them with the oil, paprika and salt and pepper in a large bowl. Place the potato wedges on a lightly greased grill set about 4 to 6 inches (10–15 cm) above the fire. Cook the potatoes, turning and basting them with a little additional oil, every 5 minutes, until they are crisp and cooked through. Serve with the chili sauce.

Potato Wafer Club Sandwich

MAKES 4 SERVINGS

4 large baking potatoes, peeled

1/2 cup (125 mL) extra virgin olive oil

1 head leaf lettuce, rinsed, dried

3 large tomatoes, thinly sliced

4 slices cooked back bacon

1 lb (500 g) cooked chicken or turkey, thinly sliced

2 ripe avocados, peeled, thinly sliced

Using a mandoline, slice the potatoes lengthwise as thinly as possible. As you work, place the potato slices in a bowl holding the olive oil. When all potatoes have been sliced, combine them well with the oil. Preheat a cast-iron pan or griddle. Lay the potato slices on the hot griddle in one layer (don't crowd them) and fry, turning frequently, until the potato slices are golden brown and beginning to crisp round the edges, about 10 minutes. Keep the cooked slices warm as you fry the others. Have all the other ingredients ready for assembly. Place a slice of potato on a serving plate, add a leaf or two of lettuce and a tomato slice and then another slice of potato. Add a slice of back bacon and chicken and another slice of potato. Top with more lettuce and avocado and another slice of potato. Serve immediately with remaining potato slices on the side.

Using ultra-thin slices of potato in place of bread makes for one inspired creation that I first enjoyed years ago at a little restaurant in New York City. They didn't call it a sandwich, but I couldn't help but think how sandwich-like it was, combined with all the traditional club sandwich ingredients. You will need a mandoline for this recipe, as the potatoes must be exceedingly thin. Prepare all the potatoes ahead of time and keep them warm while you assemble each sandwich. In the winter you can bake the potato slices in a hot oven for 10 to 15 minutes, turning them once or twice. Serve with the aïoli on page 110 or with basic mayonnaise.

Corn & Potato Salad with Grape Tomatoes & Fresh Oregano

MAKES 4 TO 6 SERVINGS

The flavours of three beautiful summer-ripe vegetables combine in this easy salad that is just made to be teamed with crusty, glazed barbecued ribs.

FOR THE VINAIGRETTE:

4 tbsp (60 mL) balsamic vinegar

Salt and freshly ground pepper

2/3 cup (150 mL) extra virgin olive oil

FOR THE CORN AND POTATO MIXTURE:

1/4 cup (60 mL) butter

3 tbsp (45 mL) olive oil

1 lb (500 g) small red new potatoes, scrubbed, halved

1 lb (500 g) small white new potatoes, scrubbed, halved

2 1/2 cups (625 mL) corn kernels (about 5 ears), cooked

2 shallots, peeled, finely chopped

2 cups (500 mL) grape tomatoes, rinsed

1/2 cup (125 mL) fresh oregano leaves, torn

Salt and freshly ground pepper

1 lb (500 g) mixed salad greens

To prepare the vinaigrette, whisk together the vinegar and salt and pepper. Drizzle in the olive oil in a thin stream, continuing to whisk until the vinaigrette is slightly thickened and well blended. Adjust the seasoning. Set the vinaigrette to one side.

Melt the butter with the oil in a large skillet over medium-high heat. Add the potato halves (do this in batches if necessary) and sauté until crisp and golden, turning the potatoes in the skillet. Add the corn kernels and stir to heat through. Transfer the potatoes and corn to a large serving bowl, scraping all the bits from the skillet into the bowl. Add the shallots, grape tomatoes, oregano leaves, the reserved vinaigrette and salt and pepper. Toss to combine well. Arrange the salad greens on serving plates, top with a good portion of the corn and potato mixture and serve.

Lemon Potato
Salad with Shrimp

MAKES 6 TO 8 SERVINGS

FOR THE SALAD:

2 lbs (1 kg) small new Yukon Gold
  potatoes or other small new potatoes,
  scrubbed, quartered

Salt

1/2 lb (250 g) skinny green beans,
  stem end trimmed

1 red onion, very thinly sliced

1 lb (500 g) cooked small salad shrimp

FOR THE DRESSING:

1 egg yolk

Salt and freshly ground pepper

Zest of 1 lemon

1/4 cup (60 mL) fresh lemon juice

2 tbsp (30 mL) Dijon mustard

1/3 cup (75 mL) extra virgin olive oil

1/3 cup (75 mL) chopped fresh
  flat-leaf parsley

Place the potatoes in a large saucepan, add just enough boiling water to cover them, bring to a boil and add a little salt. Cook the potatoes for 10 to 15 minutes, or until tender. Use a slotted spoon or small sieve to retrieve them from the water, reserving it. Give the potatoes a quick rinse under cold running water and drain. Transfer them to a large mixing bowl and set to one side.

Place the beans in a sieve and plunge them into the reserved hot potato cooking water. Bring to a boil, reduce the heat and simmer for about 5 minutes. Drain the beans, rinse them under cold running water and drain. Add the beans to the potatoes, along with the onion and shrimp.

Now, prepare the dressing. Whisk together the egg yolk, salt and pepper, lemon zest and juice and mustard. Slowly drizzle in the olive oil as you continue to whisk. Adjust the seasoning and stir in the chopped parsley. Pour the dressing over the potato mixture and serve, preferably while vegetables are still a little warm.

This recipe is perfect for a lazy summer afternoon—especially if you spent part of it picking a basketful of lovely, skinny green beans and new Yukon Golds from your vegetable garden and are wondering what to do with them. Here it is: the first new Yukons cooked and treated to a lemony dressing and combined with tiny shrimp and those slender beans. Very good summer eating.

New Potatoes with Asparagus & Prosciutto

What could be better than these three ingredients together on the same plate? There is absolutely nothing sophisticated about this preparation. It relies on the seasonal freshness of the vegetables to make it special. Make this dish when the first potatoes and asparagus make their entrance and, if you can't obtain real prosciutto from Italy, look for Westphalian ham, available in European meat shops, or good quality cured ham. Serve this dish with plenty of crusty bread and butter.

MAKES 6 SERVINGS

2 lbs (1 kg) fresh asparagus	**Juice of 1 lemon**
2 lbs (1 kg) new waxy potatoes, scrubbed	**2 tbsp (30 mL) chopped fresh chives**
1/2 tsp (2 mL) salt	**Salt and freshly ground pepper**
1/4 lb (125 g) butter, melted	**1/2 lb (250 g) prosciutto**

Wash the asparagus and, using a vegetable peeler, lightly scrape the stalks, away from the tips. Trim off the lower 2 inches (5 cm) or so (use these pieces for soups, stocks, risottos or as an omelette filling). With kitchen twine, tie the asparagus in a few bundles and set to one side.

Place the potatoes in a large, deep saucepan (large enough to hold both the potatoes and the asparagus) and cover with boiling water. Bring to a boil and add the salt. Place the asparagus bundles, upright, at the side of the saucepan and cook over medium heat until the asparagus tips are tender, about 10 to 12 minutes or so. Remove the asparagus bundles from the pan, but leave the potatoes to cook until tender, a few minutes longer. Warm a large oval serving platter. When the potatoes are ready, drain well and shake the pan a few times over low heat to dry them thoroughly. Into the melted butter whisk the lemon juice, chives and a little salt and pepper. Pour most of the mixture over the drained potatoes in the saucepan, turning the potatoes carefully to coat them with the butter mixture. Pile the potatoes in the middle of the serving platter. Remove the twine from the asparagus, arrange it in bundles around the potatoes and drizzle with the remaining butter mixture. Loosely pile the prosciutto atop the asparagus and serve at once.

Frittata with New Potatoes & Mint

1/2 lb (250 g) waxy new potatoes, scrubbed

Salt

3 tbsp (45 mL) olive oil

1 onion, finely chopped

1 cup (250 mL) whole fresh mint leaves, washed, dried

1/4 cup (60 mL) chopped fresh flat-leaf parsley

8 eggs

3 tbsp (45 mL) fresh breadcrumbs

3 tbsp (45 mL) grated Parmigiano-Reggiano cheese

2 tsp (10 mL) all-purpose flour

2 tsp (10 mL) table cream

1/2 tsp (2 mL) salt

1/4 tsp (1 mL) freshly ground pepper

Place the potatoes in a saucepan and just cover them with boiling water. Bring to a boil, add a little salt, reduce the heat and cook over medium heat for about 5 to 7 minutes; don't cook the potatoes until completely tender. Drain and, when the potatoes are cool enough to handle, chop them roughly. Set to one side.

In a large ovenproof skillet, warm some of the olive oil over medium heat. Add the onion and cook until softened, about 5 minutes. Remove from the heat. Stir in the mint and parsley. Using a rubber scraper, transfer the mixture to a small bowl and wipe the skillet clean. Crack the eggs into a large mixing bowl and whisk in the breadcrumbs, cheese, flour, cream, salt and pepper. Add the reserved onion mixture and the potatoes to the egg mixture and stir. Preheat the broiler. Return the skillet to medium heat. Pour the remaining olive oil into the skillet, swirling to coat the surface. Pour in the egg mixture. Cook gently—running a narrow metal spatula around the edges of the skillet to lift the cooked egg up and allow the uncooked egg to run underneath—for 5 minutes, or until the frittata is set and cooked on the bottom.

Place the skillet 6 inches (15 cm) below the broiler. Broil the frittata for about 2 minutes, or until the top is set and golden brown. Serve immediately or cooled to room temperature, cut into squares or wedges.

Mint and new potatoes were always cooked together in my childhood home, so that's why I thought to combine them in the classic Italian open-faced omelette that makes a terrific summer lunch. Roast or grill a whole piece of back bacon to serve with this frittata, along with halves of lightly grilled beefsteak tomatoes drizzled with extra virgin olive oil and splashed with a little balsamic vinegar.

Haystack Potato Crisps with Poached Egg & Smoked Salmon

MAKES 2 SERVINGS

This satisfying little number is certainly wonderful for breakfast, but don't limit it to just that meal—it's great absolutely any time of the day or night, as far as I am concerned. This is a quick meal to make with someone you love—one of you can make the poached eggs and the other the potato crisps, and together you can assemble and enjoy this dish. No matter how you cut it, everyone's a winner. If another hungry couple invades, just double the recipe, and if you're chicken about poaching eggs, scrambled or fried eggs will work just fine.

2 large baking potatoes, peeled
1 shallot, peeled
3 tbsp (45 mL) melted butter
Salt and freshly ground pepper

3 tbsp (45 mL) olive oil
1/4 lb (125 g) smoked salmon, sliced
2 large eggs, poached

Grate the potatoes and shallot onto a clean tea towel. Gather up the ends and, over the sink, twist together to wring out any moisture. Transfer the potato mixture to a bowl and toss with the melted butter and some salt and pepper. Gloss the surface of a skillet with a little of the olive oil and place over medium-high heat. When the pan is hot, add spoonfuls of the potato mixture, flattened considerably with a metal spatula, and cook until really crisp and deep golden brown. Transfer the potato crisps to warmed plates. To assemble, top a potato crisp with a piece of smoked salmon, add another potato crisp and another piece of salmon, and crown with a poached egg. Add a good grind of pepper and serve immediately.

Caesar's Spuds

MAKES 4 TO 6 SERVINGS

FOR THE POTATOES:

2 lbs (1 kg) small new waxy
    potatoes, scrubbed

1 tsp (5 mL) salt

FOR THE DRESSING:

2–3 anchovy fillets, drained

2 cloves garlic, crushed

1 large egg yolk

3 tbsp (45 mL) white wine vinegar

2 tbsp (30 mL) fresh lemon juice

1 tbsp (15 mL) Dijon mustard

1 cup (250 mL) extra virgin olive oil

1/2 cup (125 mL) vegetable oil

Salt and freshly ground pepper

6 slices bacon, fried until crisp, chopped

1 cup (250 mL) grated Parmesan cheese

1/2 cup (125 mL) fresh flat-leaf parsley,
    rinsed, dried, finely chopped

Hearts of romaine lettuce

Place the potatoes in a large saucepan and just cover them with boiling water. Bring to a boil, add the salt and cook until the potatoes are tender, about 15 to 20 minutes.

Meanwhile, prepare the dressing. In a food processor or blender, combine the anchovies, garlic, egg yolk, vinegar, lemon juice and mustard. Pulse on and off a few times to blend the ingredients and then, with the motor running, gradually add the oils in a stream to make a thick dressing. Season with salt and pepper and transfer the mixture to a covered container.

When the potatoes are cooked, drain and let them cool slightly. Cut them into halves or rough chunks and transfer to a mixing bowl. Pour enough of the dressing over them as required to coat the potatoes well. Add the bacon, cheese and parsley and toss with the potatoes. Serve in bowls lined with romaine lettuce leaves.

Like every man and boy I know, my dearest love adores Caesar salad. Left to his own devices, I'm sure he would enjoy one every evening with his dinner. But because I need potatoes almost as much as I need him, I figured if I put Caesar salad and potatoes together, we'd both be very happy. And we are. My invention is wonderful with steaks, bacon cheeseburgers or just about anything at all. If you have more dressing than you need, place it in a container, refrigerate and use the next day.

Red Potatoes & Grilled Mustard Chicken with Yellow Tomatoes

MAKES 6 TO 8 SERVINGS

Just when you thought you couldn't face another boneless chicken breast, summer comes along and brings all the good things that make them taste new again. Vary the tomatoes and peppers (red, yellow) and the greens (arugula, frisée).

2 lbs (1 kg) small red potatoes, scrubbed

Salt

1 lb (500 g) snowpeas or sugar snap peas

3/4 cup (175 mL) extra virgin olive oil

1/4 cup (60 mL) dry white wine

6 boneless, skinless chicken breasts

Salt and freshly ground pepper

3 tbsp + 1 tbsp (45 mL + 15 mL)
   Dijon mustard

Juice of 1 small lemon

1 clove garlic, minced

1/4 cup (60 mL) chopped fresh basil

2 cups (500 mL) yellow pear
   tomatoes, halved

1 yellow bell pepper, seeded, thinly sliced

3 cups (750 mL) baby spinach leaves

Place the potatoes in a large saucepan, cover them with boiling water, bring to a boil and add a little salt. Reduce the heat and cook until the potatoes are tender, about 15 minutes. Remove the potatoes from the cooking water with a slotted spoon, reserving the water. Rinse them under cold running water, drain and set to one side.

Plunge the peas into the potato cooking water, bring to a boil and cook just until crisp-tender, 1 minute for snowpeas, 3 minutes for sugar snap peas. Drain, rinse them under cold running water and drain again. Set to one side.

Preheat the grill to medium-high. Whisk together the olive oil and white wine. Brush about half of this mixture onto the chicken breasts. Season them with salt and pepper and spread the 3 tablespoons (45 mL) mustard over them. Grill the chicken breasts for about 4 to 5 minutes per side, or until cooked through, brushing the oil mixture on them from time to time as they cook. Remove the chicken breasts from the grill and let cool on a plate. Into the remaining oil mixture whisk the lemon juice, garlic, basil and the 1 tablespoon (15 mL) mustard, along with a little salt and pepper. Adjust the seasoning and set the dressing to one side.

Slice the chicken breasts into thick strips and place them in a large bowl with the potatoes, peas, tomato halves and bell pepper. Arrange the spinach leaves on a large serving platter. Give the dressing a good whisk and pour it over the chicken and potato mixture, tossing to combine well. Arrange the chicken and potato mixture over the spinach leaves and serve.

 Two words commonly found in the English lexicon came to us by way of the Irish and the potato. It was the Irish who first referred to potatoes as "spuds," a name that derived from the type of spade used in their cultivation. The pot used to cook potatoes in Ireland was usually lifted away from the fire and set into the ground, enabling the cook to mash the potatoes without getting burned by the hot pot. Over time and repeated mashings, the hot pot would form a deep well in the ground—the pothole.

Crisp Potato Pakoras with Mint & Cilantro Chutney

MAKES 4 SERVINGS

Fans of Indian food know all about pakoras, the crisp little fritters composed of vegetables such as spinach and onion and, best of all, potato. Pakoras are quite easy to prepare and make great hors d'oeuvres before a summer barbecue. Be sure to get the oil hot enough to ensure that the inside of the potato is cooked and the exterior is crunchy-crisp. Look for chickpea flour in Indian food shops, where it may also be labelled besan. As chickpea flour is used extensively in Sicilian cuisine, you may also find it in some Italian supermarkets or food shops.

FOR THE CHUTNEY:
2 cups (500 mL) fresh mint leaves
1 cup (250 mL) fresh chopped cilantro
1/2 cup (125 mL) dried coconut
1/4 cup (60 mL) water
2 tbsp (30 mL) fresh lime juice
1 tsp (5 mL) brown sugar
1 tsp (5 mL) salt
1/2 tsp (2 mL) hot red pepper flakes
2 tsp (10 mL) canola or other vegetable oil

FOR THE PAKORA BATTER:
1 cup (250 mL) chickpea flour
2 tbsp (30 mL) rice flour
1 tbsp (15 mL) fresh lime juice
1/2 tsp (2 mL) chili powder
1/2 tsp (2 mL) salt
1/2 tsp (2 mL) turmeric
1/2 cup (125 mL) water
1/8 tsp (.5 mL) baking soda

FOR THE POTATOES:
Vegetable oil
3 large baking potatoes, peeled, sliced
1/8-inch (3 mm) thick

First, make the chutney. Place all the chutney ingredients, except the oil, in a blender or food processor. Using the pulse motion, purée the ingredients until smooth. Heat the oil in a small saucepan over medium heat. Add the chutney mixture (be wary of the oil spitting) and stir-fry for 10 minutes until the mixture becomes fragrant. Scrape it into a little bowl and let cool. Cover with plastic wrap and chill until ready to serve with the pakoras.

Sift the chickpea and rice flour together into a mixing bowl. Add the lime juice, chili powder, salt and turmeric and then slowly add the water, whisking it into the the flour mixture. Keep whisking the batter until it is like heavy cream. Cover the bowl and let sit for 10 minutes.

Warm the oven. Place about 3 inches (8 cm) oil in a deep-fryer or similar heavy pot and heat to 360°F (185°C). If you are not using a deep-fryer, use a candy thermometer to gauge the temperature of the oil. As it is heating, add the baking soda to the batter and beat for a minute or so. Dip the potato slices in the batter, letting the excess drip back into the bowl, and carefully slip them into the hot oil. Repeat until you have about 6 slices in the oil. Fry for about 5 minutes until golden on both sides, turning the potato slices with a slotted spoon once or twice. Once cooked, transfer them to a paper towel–lined baking sheet and keep them warm in the oven. Serve with the chutney.

 In the legendary cookbook *Mrs. Beeton's Everyday Cookery,* published in the early 1900s, the British doyenne of the kitchen wrote about the humble spud, heading up the section "Potato as Food" with: "No doubt much of its popularity is due to its cheapness, its good keeping power, and its unobtrusive flavour."

Penne with Potatoes & Arugula

MAKES 4 SERVINGS

Pasta may not be the first thing you think to team with potatoes—or vice versa—but there is something intrinsically good about these two comfort foods together in one dish: similar textures, yet distinctly different shapes. In this dish, one complements the other and each is flavourfully supported by peppery arugula and a hit of red onion. This recipe is easily doubled and requires precooking the potatoes in a hot oven. If you're preparing this in the summer months and are loath to turn on the oven, grill or pan-fry the potato slices until crisp.

1 lb (500 g) waxy new potatoes, scrubbed, sliced

1/2 cup (125 mL) extra virgin olive oil

Salt and freshly ground pepper

1 lb (500 g) orecchiette (little ear-shaped pasta)

Salt

1 small red onion, very thinly sliced

4 cloves garlic, finely chopped

1 sprig fresh lemon thyme (or other lemon herb), leaves finely chopped

2 bunches fresh arugula (about 1/2 lb/ 250 g), rinsed, dried

Juice of 1 small lemon

Zest of 1 lemon, finely chopped

1 cup (250 mL) freshly grated Parmigiano-Reggiano cheese

Preheat the oven to 400°F (200°C). Toss potatoes with some of the olive oil and season with salt and pepper. Transfer the potatoes to a baking sheet and roast in the oven until crispy and golden brown, about 15 minutes. When done, remove the potatoes from the oven and set to one side.

Bring a large pot of water to a boil on a high heat. Add the pasta and a little salt, stir and cook the pasta until tender but still firm; don't overcook.

While the pasta is cooking, place a little more of the olive oil in a skillet and sauté the onion until soft, about 4 minutes. Add the potatoes, garlic and lemon thyme and toss for a minute or so to combine. Drain the pasta (do not rinse) and add it to the potatoes, along with the arugula. Add the lemon juice and zest and the rest of the olive oil and toss together. Sprinkle on the cheese and serve.

English Country Garden Herb & Potato Salad

MAKES 4 TO 6 SERVINGS

2 1/2 lbs (1.25 kg) small waxy
   potatoes, scrubbed
Salt
1/2 cup (125 mL) extra virgin olive oil
3 tbsp (45 mL) white wine vinegar
Salt and freshly ground pepper
1/2 cup (125 mL) finely chopped
   fresh chives

1/2 cup (125 mL) finely chopped
   fresh dill
1/2 cup (125 mL) finely chopped
   fresh parsley
1/2 cup (125 mL) finely chopped
   fresh tarragon

Place the potatoes in a saucepan and just cover them with boiling water. Add a little salt and bring to a boil. Cook for 15 to 20 minutes, or until the potatoes are tender right through when tested with the tip of a knife; don't overcook. As the potatoes are cooking, whisk together the olive oil, vinegar and salt and pepper in a large mixing bowl. When the potatoes are cooked, drain and let them cool just enough so that you can handle them. Working quickly, peel the skins from the potatoes with a little paring knife and add the potatoes to the olive oil mixture, tossing gently to coat them with the dressing. Add the chopped herbs and toss again, adding a little more olive oil or vinegar, if necessary. Serve immediately.

I was once served a deliciously fragrant warm potato salad in a lovely old walled garden in southwest England, the potatoes and herbs having been picked an hour or so before I enjoyed them. This salad is wonderful served with slices of cold ham, tiny tomatoes and a few halves of hard-boiled egg— understated elegance at its British best. Vary the selection of fresh herbs as you wish.

Rösti with Fresh Herbs

For rösti—Switzerland's famed potato dish—you must begin preparation the night before you plan on serving it, or at least first thing in the morning of the same day. You need to parboil the potatoes whole, in their skins, and then allow them to sit for a time before grating them. It's easy to improvise with this dish (as I have done here), adding different herbs or ingredients from the onion family (shallots, leeks, chives) as you wish. Of course, you could throw caution to the wind and also include a whole lot of cooked, crumbled bacon, but you didn't hear that from me. Sliced tomatoes go well with rösti, too.

MAKES 4 TO 6 SERVINGS

6 evenly sized baking potatoes, scrubbed
Salt
1 medium red onion, minced
1/2 cup (125 mL) chopped fresh
  flat-leaf parsley
1/4 cup (60 mL) chopped fresh sage
Salt and freshly ground pepper
4 tbsp (60 mL) unsalted butter
2 tbsp (30 mL) olive oil

Place the potatoes in a large pot, just cover them with cold water and bring to a boil. Add a little salt, bring back to a boil and cook the potatoes over medium heat for about 12 to 15 minutes. Test the potatoes with the tip of a knife; they should still be quite firm at the centre. Drain and rinse the potatoes under cold water. Refrigerate them overnight or for at least 6 hours.

When ready to make the rösti, peel the potatoes and, using either a large-holed grater or a food processor fitted with the shredding/grating disk, shred the potatoes. Transfer them to a mixing bowl and combine them with the onion, parsely, sage and salt and pepper, mixing together well. In a 12-inch (30 cm), preferably nonstick skillet, heat half the butter and half the olive oil over medium-high heat. Add all of the potato mixture, spread it evenly over the pan using a metal spatula and press down firmly. (At this point, some cooks add more butter, but I'll leave that to your discretion.) Cook over medium heat until the bottom of the rösti is cooked and golden brown. Remove the pan from the heat, place a large plate over the pan and invert so that the rösti slips out onto the plate. Return the pan to the heat, add the remaining butter and oil and reheat over medium-high heat. Slide the rösti, uncooked side down, back into the pan and, pressing the rösti down with the spatula, cook the other side until it is golden brown, another 10 minutes or so. Turn the rösti out onto a heated platter, cut into wedges and serve.

 Of potatoes and presidents ... Former U.S. president Bill Clinton loved the Yukon Gold potato so much that he instructed the White House cooks to serve it rather than other potatoes while he was in office. Before John Adams became the second president of the United States, he mentioned potatoes in a letter written to his wife in reference to his nation's struggle for independence from Britain: "Let us eat potatoes and drink water, let us wear canvas, and undressed sheepskins, rather than submit to the unrighteous and ignominious domination that is prepared for us." George Washington had the potato planted on his estate in 1767, and Thomas Jefferson wrote about spuds in his journal in 1794.

Smoked Haddock with Yukon Golds in Mustard Beurre Blanc

MAKES 4 SERVINGS

This is a pleasing, light lunch or supper dish just right for a warm summer day when you want something a little richer or more substantial than a simple salad but less demanding than meat. This preparation will also work well with fillets of salmon or trout in place of the smoked haddock, if you prefer. (While the amount of butter seems high, remember that beurre blanc is the classic French butter sauce, "butter" being the operative word.)

FOR THE POTATOES:
2 lbs (1 kg) small or baby Yukon Gold potatoes, scrubbed
Salt

FOR THE BEURRE BLANC:
2 shallots, peeled, minced
2 tbsp (30 mL) dry white wine
2 tbsp (30 mL) white wine vinegar

1 tbsp (15 mL) heavy cream
1/2 lb (8 oz/250 g) cold, unsalted butter, diced
Salt and freshly ground pepper
1 tbsp (15 mL) whole grain mustard

FOR THE FISH:
4 7-oz (200 g) pieces smoked haddock
2 cups (500 mL) whole milk, warmed (approx.)
Sprigs of fresh chervil or flat-leaf parsley

Place the potatoes in a saucepan, cover them with boiling water, add a little salt and cook until tender, about 15 to 20 minutes.

As the potatoes are cooking, prepare the beurre blanc, bearing in mind that it must be kept warm for serving. Half fill a medium-sized saucepan with hot water and keep hot on medium-high heat. Combine the shallots, wine and vinegar in a small saucepan and cook quickly for a minute or so, until reduced and thickened. Add the cream and reduce a little more. Set the saucepan over the larger one half-filled with very hot (not boiling) water. Now, add the diced cold butter, bit by bit, beating with a wire whisk as you work, eventually incorporating all the butter. When the sauce is thick, season with salt and pepper and stir in the mustard, whisking to blend well. Reduce the heat to low, cover the small saucepan with a lid and keep warm set within the larger saucepan.

Drain the potatoes and let them cool slightly. Peel the potatoes, slice them and keep warm.

To prepare the fish, place the smoked haddock in a shallow pan and pour in just enough of the milk to cover. Bring to a gentle boil, reduce the heat and cook for about 5 to 7 minutes, depending on the thickness of the fish, until the fish is opaque. Carefully drain the fish, discarding the cooking liquid. Cover the fish and keep warm.

To serve, arrange a portion of sliced potatoes on a warm plate, cover with some of the beurre blanc and top with a portion of fish and more beurre blanc. Serve at once with a sprig of fresh chervil or parsley.

 Never store potatoes and onions together or near each other. Onions give off a specific gas that helps to speed up the rotting process in potatoes. One good method of storing potatoes is in discarded pantyhose! Drop a few potatoes in one leg and hang in a cool, dry, dark place. The pantyhose will allow air to circulate, an all-important factor in the successful storage of potatoes.

Potatoes for comfort and to help drive the cold winter away, as the song goes. As the days grow shorter and colder and the wintry nights descend, the potato really comes into its own in terms of versatility and real eating satisfaction. From substantial soups, starters and appetizers to breads, stews, slow-cooked sides and no end of main course dishes, you'll find something here to fill every wintry bill.

the winter potato

Twice-Baked Potato Soufflé with Cashel Blue Cheese

MAKES 4 SERVINGS

Cashel blue is a blue-veined cheese from Ireland and one of my favourites. You can use any blue cheese you like for this easy first course. These are not delicate, fragile little soufflés, but rather the more substantial version that receives an initial baking and then another, topped with extra cheese. You can do the first baking ahead of time and the final one just before serving. Great for company, these little soufflés go well with lightly dressed salad greens or more baby spinach.

3 medium floury potatoes, peeled

Salt

3 eggs, separated

1/2 cup (125 mL) all-purpose flour

3/4 tsp (3 mL) baking powder

1/4 tsp (1 mL) salt

1/2 lb (250 g) Cashel blue cheese, crumbled

Salt and freshly ground pepper

1 cup (250 mL) loosely packed baby spinach leaves, finely chopped

4 tsp (20 mL) butter

Preheat the oven to 400°F (200°C). Cut the potatoes into rough chunks, place them in a saucepan and just cover them with cold water. Bring to a boil, add a little salt and boil until the potatoes are quite tender. Drain them thoroughly and shake the saucepan a few times over the heat to dry them thoroughly.

Remove the saucepan from the heat and mash the potatoes, adding the egg yolks as you do. In a bowl, combine the flour with the baking powder and the 1/4 teaspoon (1 mL) salt, whisking them together well. Add half of the cheese and all of the flour mixture to the mashed potatoes, blending to combine the ingredients well. Season with a little salt and pepper. Fold the spinach into the potato mixture. Set to one side.

In a mixing bowl, whip the egg whites until they form soft peaks. Gently fold the egg whites into the potato mixture, being careful not to overblend. Grease 4 ramekins with the butter. Divide the mixture among the ramekins. Place them on a baking sheet and bake for 20 minutes.

Remove the ramekins from the oven and let cool. When ready to serve, cover a baking sheet with parchment paper and turn the soufflés out of the ramekins onto the lined baking sheet. Distribute the remaining cheese over the soufflés and return them to the oven, this time for about 5 minutes. Serve.

Super Spud Skins
with Smokin' Chili

MAKES 4 TO 6 SERVINGS

2 tbsp (30 mL) olive oil

1 lb (500 g) lean ground beef

1/2 lb (250 g) lean ground pork

2 cloves garlic, chopped

1 large onion, peeled, chopped

1–2 small fresh red chiles, finely chopped

1 tbsp (15 mL) ground ancho chile (optional)

1 heaping tbsp (20 mL) cumin

1 tbsp (15 mL) dried oregano

2 tsp (10 mL) cayenne pepper (or to taste)

4 cups (1 L) canned plum tomatoes (with juice), chopped

4 tbsp (60 mL) tomato paste

Salt and freshly ground pepper

4 large baking potatoes, scrubbed

1/2 cup (125 mL) chopped fresh cilantro

1 cup (250 mL) sour cream

Pour the olive oil into a large saucepan or skillet and add the ground meats. Stir together over medium-high heat, breaking up the meat. Once the meat is browned, pour off most of the fat. Add the garlic, onion, red chiles, ground ancho chile, cumin, oregano and cayenne and stir to blend well. Cook for a few minutes and add the chopped tomatoes and their juice. Bring the mixture to a boil and cook for 10 minutes. Add the tomato paste and stir it into the meat mixture well. Season with salt and pepper. Simmer the chili for about 1 hour over low heat.

Preheat the oven to 425°F (220°C). Bake the potatoes directly on the top rack for at least 1 hour; an extra 10 to 15 minutes won't hurt either. When the potatoes are done, remove them from the oven and let cool until you can handle them. Cut the potatoes in half crosswise, scoop out the flesh and add it to the chili, stirring it in well. Arrange the potato skins on a plate. Stir the cilantro into the chili and scoop the mixture into the potato skins. Top each with a little sour cream and serve.

We don't often put potatoes and chili together, but I don't know why not; they seem pretty natural bedfellows to me. If you have a chili recipe of which you are particularly fond, by all means use it here. If not, this version is a good basic one. This meaty chili contains no beans, but feel free to add some if you wish. This dish can be enjoyed as an appetizer, a snack or a full meal, depending on how many people you are serving. Make the chili the day before you plan to serve it. The next day, stick the potatoes in the oven and head out for a winter walk. Great fare for a busy winter weekend.

Fish Pie with Thatched Potatoes

MAKES 4 TO 6 SERVINGS

A friend of mine in the north of England always called the mashed potato mixture that she used to top fish pies a "thatch." Whatever you call it, crowning soft, creamy compositions of white-sauced fish with a cloud of fluffy mash results in a dish that is just about as good as it gets on the comfort-food scale. I love salmon in these pies, but you may use any firm-fleshed fish (cod, haddock, hake, halibut) you like, or a combination.

FOR THE FISH:
1 lb (500 g) cod fillets
1/2 lb (250 g) salmon fillets
4 sprigs fresh flat-leaf parsley
2 sprigs fresh thyme
2 whole black peppercorns
2-inch (5 cm) piece lemon peel
3 tbsp (45 mL) dry white wine
Salt and freshly ground pepper
3 green onions, trimmed, very
 finely chopped
1/4 cup (60 mL) chopped fresh
 flat-leaf parsley

FOR THE POTATOES:
2 lbs (1 kg) floury potatoes,
 peeled, quartered
Salt
2/3 cup (150 mL) whole milk
2 tbsp (30 mL) butter

FOR THE SAUCE:
2 tbsp (30 mL) butter
3 tbsp (45 mL) all-purpose flour
2/3 cup (150 mL) whole milk
Salt and freshly ground pepper

Place the fish in a large skillet, along with the parsley sprigs, thyme, pepper-corns, lemon peel, wine and salt and pepper. Add just enough water to cover the fish fillets, bring to a boil, reduce the heat to low and poach the fish for 15 minutes. Don't allow the liquid to boil. Carefully drain the fish, retaining the cooking liquid. Pour the liquid through a sieve and discard the solids. Set the liquid and fish to one side.

Preheat the oven to 400°F (200°C). Place the potatoes in a large saucepan, cover them with cold water and bring to a boil. Add a little salt and cook until the potatoes are tender.

While the potatoes are cooking, prepare the sauce. Melt the butter in a saucepan over low heat. Whisk in the flour and cook gently for about a minute. Gradually add 2/3 cup (150 mL) of the fish cooking liquid and the milk to the flour mixture, whisking well after each addition to keep lumps from forming. Simmer for 5 minutes or so, whisking now and then, until the white sauce thickens (if it is too thick, add a little more milk). Season with salt and pepper. Remove from the heat and set to one side for a moment.

Drain the potatoes well and return the saucepan to the heat to dry them thoroughly, shaking the pan over the heat a few times. Mash the potatoes with the milk and butter and stir vigorously with a wooden spoon to incorporate a little air into the mash. Cover and set to one side.

When the fish is cool enough to handle, break it up into chunks with your fingers, discarding any skin or bones. Lightly butter a large baking dish and place the chunks of fish in it, distributing them evenly. Scatter the chopped onion and parsley over the fish. Now, give the reserved white sauce a good whisk and pour it over the fish. Cover with the mashed potatoes, spreading them evenly over the sauced fish. Bake for about 30 minutes, until the sauce begins to bubble round the edges and the potatoes are golden brown and forming crisp peaks.

Lamb Shoulder with Potatoes & Tomatoes

MAKES 6 SERVINGS

This good, warming dish demonstrates the compatibility of lamb and potatoes in the same dish. In Greece and Italy, these two foods are often combined with great success. A breeze to put together, this recipe is a perfect example of their marriage. Fresh or canned tomatoes will work well here. Serve this dish with a green vegetable and crusty bread and butter.

2 lbs (1 kg) lamb shoulder, cut into chunks

1 lb (500 g) Yukon Gold potatoes, peeled, cut into chunks

4 cups (1 L) peeled, chopped plum tomatoes

4 tbsp (60 mL) extra virgin olive oil

Zest of 1 lemon, finely chopped

2 cloves garlic, chopped

2 sprigs fresh rosemary

1 large onion, thinly sliced

1/4 cup (60 mL) chopped fresh flat-leaf parsley

2 tsp (10 mL) dried oregano

Salt and freshly ground pepper

Preheat the oven to 350°F (180°C). Combine the lamb and the potatoes in a large terra cotta (or similar moisture-retaining) baking dish with a lid. Place the tomatoes in a bowl and add the olive oil, lemon zest, garlic, rosemary, onion, parsley and oregano. Toss together to combine well and season with salt and pepper. Distribute this mixture over the lamb and drizzle a little more olive oil over all. Cover and bake for about 2 hours; by then the potatoes and lamb should both be quite tender.

Winter Warmer Potato Salad

MAKES 6 TO 8 SERVINGS

3 lbs (1.5 kg) Yukon Gold potatoes
  (or other all-purpose potatoes), peeled

2 tbsp (30 mL) caraway seeds

Salt

1 onion, chopped

1/2 cup (125 mL) vegetable or chicken broth

5 tbsp (75 mL) white wine vinegar

1 tsp (5 mL) sugar

Salt and freshly ground pepper

4 tbsp (60 mL) vegetable oil

1/4 cup (60 mL) chopped fresh
  flat-leaf parsley

Place the whole potatoes and caraway seeds in a large saucepan. Cover the potatoes with cold water, bring to a boil over high heat and add a little salt. Cook until the potatoes are tender, about 20 to 25 minutes. To drain potatoes, pour them through a sieve (to catch any caraway seeds). Pass them quickly under cold running water and drain well again. Slice the potatoes directly into a large bowl and add the collected caraway seeds. Scatter the onion over the potatoes, warm the broth and pour it directly over the vegetables. In a measuring cup, whisk the vinegar with the sugar, salt and pepper and pour over the potato mixture. Combine gently with the potato mixture and set to one side for about 20 minutes. Just before serving, drizzle the oil over the potatoes and scatter the parsley over all. Mix together once more and serve.

On a cycling tour of wine country in Germany's Mosel region, I must have enjoyed this kartoffelsalat *at least once a day. Although this preparation is not really a salad in the strict sense of the term, it is very good with any pork, whether in the form of a roast, sausages, ham or other cured pork product. You might even add a bit of smoked bacon to the salad itself and serve sided with cucumbers and onions in sour cream with dill. Use vegetable or chicken bouillon cubes for the broth.*

Potato Griddle Scones

Wait until you taste these lovely little griddle-cooked scones that are based on mashed potato and Cheddar. It's difficult to say when and how you will enjoy them best— at breakfast, lunch or dinner, as a snack, an appetizer or party pieces, dolled up with smoked salmon or any number of other toppings. Make a batch for the two of you to enjoy in front of the fire with lashings of butter. Use a cast-iron skillet or griddle to cook these scones and serve them with butter, salt and pepper.

2 large floury potatoes, peeled, cut into chunks

Salt

1 cup (250 mL) all-purpose flour

1 1/2 tsp (7 mL) baking powder

1 tsp (5 mL) dry mustard

1/2 tsp (2 mL) salt

1 egg, beaten

2/3 cup (150 mL) whole milk

1/2 cup (125 mL) old white Cheddar cheese

1 tbsp (15 mL) chopped fresh flat-leaf parsley

Salt and freshly ground pepper

3 tbsp (45 mL) vegetable oil

Place the potatoes in a saucepan, cover them with cold water, bring to a boil, add a little salt and cook until tender. Drain the potatoes well and place on low heat to dry them thoroughly, shaking the pan over the heat a few times. Using a potato masher, dry mash the potatoes and transfer them to a mixing bowl. Blend the flour with the baking powder, mustard and 1/2 teaspoon (2 mL) salt and add the mixture to the mashed potato, along with the egg, milk, cheese and parsley. Using a wooden spoon, beat this mixture to incorporate all the ingredients well. Season with a little salt and pepper.

Using a pastry brush, gloss the surface of a cast-iron skillet or griddle with a little oil. Drop large spoonfuls (not too much) of the batter onto the pan, give each a slight pat with a metal spatula, and cook for 1 to 2 minutes. Flip the scones and cook the other side for the same length of time. Transfer them to a baking sheet as they are cooked, keep warm and repeat with remaining mixture. Serve right away.

Fennel, Potato & White Bean Stew

MAKES 4 TO 6 SERVINGS

1/2 lb (250 g) dried white beans

1 lb (500 g) red-skinned potatoes,
   scrubbed, halved

1/4 cup (60 mL) extra virgin olive oil

2 bulbs fennel, trimmed, cored, thinly sliced,
   fronds reserved

2 carrots, finely chopped

1 large white onion, finely chopped

4 cloves garlic, crushed

1 tsp (5 mL) curry powder

4 cups (1 L) vegetable broth or light
   chicken broth

4 fresh or canned plum tomatoes,
   peeled, chopped

To quick-soak the dried beans, rinse them, place them in a large bowl and cover with boiling water. Let stand for 10 minutes, drain and repeat the process. While the beans are soaking, steam (or boil) the potatoes until they are just tender when tested with the tip of a knife. When they are cool enough to handle, slice the potatoes thickly. Set to one side.

Warm the olive oil in a large saucepan over medium heat and cook the fennel, carrots and onion for 12 minutes, or until just soft. Add the garlic and curry powder and cook for a few minutes, stirring all the ingredients together. Add the drained beans and broth, bring to a boil, reduce the heat and simmer for about 1 hour, or until the beans are tender, being careful not to overcook.

Add the potatoes and tomatoes and simmer over medium heat until the potatoes are heated through. Serve immediately, garnished with some finely chopped fennel fronds.

There is no meat—and none is needed—in this fragrant, earthy dish that combines many full-flavoured vegetables with a little Indian spice to make it winter worthy. When trimming fennel, reserve the feathery fronds to use as a finely chopped garnish. Serve with a rice pilau or squares of set polenta and chunks of Parmigiano-Reggiano.

Potato & Cheese Custard Tart

This is a bit of a wow dish, even though it consists of a series of simple, everyday ingredients. Somehow, when they all come together, housed within golden pastry, the whole is quite impressive. If you have a pastry recipe that you rely on, use it here, or try this one, which is based on unsalted butter. Inspired by the tarts composed of similar ingredients that abound in countryside bakeries in France, this one is lovely with hearty sausages cooked with red wine and onions and an accompanying salad of sharp, peppery greens dressed in a mustard vinaigrette. Ooh-la-la!

MAKES 6 TO 8 SERVINGS

FOR THE PASTRY SHELL:
2 cups (500 mL) all-purpose flour
1/4 tsp (1 mL) salt
1/3 lb (175 g) unsalted butter
1/3 cup (75 mL) ice water

FOR THE POTATO FILLING:
2 large baking potatoes, peeled
Salt
2 tbsp (30 mL) butter
Salt and freshly ground pepper
1 extra large egg
1/2 cup (125 mL) heavy cream
1/4 lb (125 g) Gruyère cheese, grated

Combine the flour and salt in a mixing bowl and cut in the butter in pieces. When the mixture is crumbly, add the ice water and mix to form a dough. Wrap it in plastic wrap and chill for about 1 hour. On a lightly floured surface, roll out the dough and cut it to fit a 10-inch (25 cm) pie or flan pan. Line the pan with the pastry and set to one side.

Preheat the oven to 375°F (190°C). Using a mandoline or sharp chef's knife, slice the potatoes very thinly. Place the slices in cold water in a saucepan as you work. When all the potatoes are sliced and just covered with cold water, bring to a boil and add a little salt. Reduce the heat and parboil the potatoes for about 5 minutes. Drain them well, transfer to a clean tea towel and pat dry.

Arrange the potatoes in an overlapping pattern to cover the bottom of the pastry. Dot the surface with a little of the butter, seasoning with a little salt and pepper as you work. Repeat to form 2 more layers of potatoes, butter and seasoning. Now, cover the tart with foil and bake for 45 minutes, or until the potatoes are tender. Whisk together the egg and cream. Remove the tart from the oven and pour the cream mixture over the potatoes. Scatter the cheese over the surface.

Carefully return the tart to the oven and bake for about 20 minutes, or until the filling has set and the surface is beginning to turn golden brown. Remove from oven and let sit for a few minutes before serving.

 Cutting potatoes too long before cooking them can result in discoloration. To avoid this, dip the cut potato in cool, acidulated water (water to which you have added a few tablespoons of lemon juice). After dipping them, drain, cover and refrigerate the potatoes until ready to use. If cut potatoes have discoloured, simmering them in milk will whiten them.

Mennonite Country Potato Doughnuts

MAKES ABOUT 3 1/2 DOZEN

1 cup (250 mL) warm mashed potatoes

2 eggs

1 cup (250 mL) buttermilk

2/3 cup (150 mL) white sugar

1 tbsp (15 mL) pure vanilla extract

2 tbsp (30 mL) butter, melted

4 cups (1 L) all-purpose flour

2 tsp (10 mL) baking powder

2 tsp (10 mL) nutmeg

1 tsp (5 mL) baking soda

1 tsp (5 mL) salt

6 cups (1.5 L) vegetable oil

Icing sugar (optional)

When my daughters were small, we used to make the yearly trek to the Mennonite Relief Sale and Fair held in New Hamburg, Ontario. What an eat fest! Arriving in the early morning meant you started with the homemade sausage and pancake brekkie. Later on, after walking round to see the sights and take in the beautiful handmade quilt auction action, you might settle down with a paper plate of outstanding charcoal barbecued chicken with creamy coleslaw and, for dessert, fresh strawberry pie with cream. One year, just in case we got hungry on the way home, we nabbed a bag of potato doughnuts, rich, moist and unforgettable. These are very close.

Place the potatoes in a large mixing bowl and blend in the eggs, together with the buttermilk, sugar, vanilla and melted butter. In another bowl, sift together the flour, baking powder, nutmeg, baking soda and salt. Add the dry ingredients to the potato mixture gradually, stirring well after each addition until well incorporated, adding a little more flour, if necessary, to form a dough. Separate the dough into 2 balls and cover with plastic wrap. Chill until the dough is easy to handle.

When the dough is ready, begin to heat the oil in a deep-fryer or other heavy, deep pot. If you are not using a deep-fryer, use a candy thermometer to gauge the temperature of the oil. Roll the dough out about 3/4-inch (2 cm) thick. Flour a biscuit cutter and cut doughnuts (don't twist the cutter) out of the dough. Use another quite small cutter to cut out holes (or leave the dough in circles rather than rings). When the temperature reaches 375°F (190°C), fry no more than 3 doughnuts at a time until golden brown, about 2 to 3 minutes. Flip them and fry until golden brown on the other side. Continue the process until all the doughnuts are cooked. Serve them sprinkled with the icing sugar, if using.

Potato Noodles

6 large floury potatoes, scrubbed, halved	1 tbsp (15 mL) salt
Salt	2–3 cups (500–750 mL) all-purpose flour
1 egg + 1 egg yolk	1/3 cup (75 mL) butter

Place the potatoes in a large saucepan, cover them with cold water, bring to a boil and add a little salt. Cook until the potatoes are tender, about 20 minutes. Drain the potatoes and, when cool enough to handle, peel them. Return the potatoes to the pot and shake over low heat until they are quite dry. Mash them with a potato masher. Cool, then cover the mashed potato and refrigerate overnight.

To make the noodles, combine the whole egg and egg yolk and add them, together with the 1 tablespoon (15 mL) salt, to the mashed potatoes in a large mixing bowl. Mix the flour into the mashed potato mixture a bit at a time until a smooth dough is formed and can be handled and kneaded without sticking. You may not need all the flour. On a lightly floured surface, shape the dough into a long roll. Slice the roll into flattish, lengthwise strips. Slice these into even thinner strips. Once all the dough has been sliced, melt the butter in a large, heavy skillet and fry the noodles for 10 to 12 minutes, or until they are beginning to get golden brown on all sides.

These rustic noodles have a great Old World flavour and style and are absolutely wonderful with any stew or with sauced preparations such as meatballs in a sour cream sauce. Or, just toss these noodles with chopped parsley and serve them with crisp, pan-fried meats like schnitzel. Cook the potatoes the day before. Mash them, cover and store in the refrigerator overnight.

Potato & Chorizo Hash with Yellow Pepper Sauce

MAKES 4 SERVINGS

Make this dish for a special winter weekend brunch or lunch to accompany a soufflé, or just serve it with poached eggs. If you can't obtain chorizo (a flavourful, spicy Spanish-style sausage), use any hard sausage in its place. Look for good quality sun-dried tomatoes packed in olive oil. If you like, use that drained olive oil in place of the olive oil in the hash.

FOR THE SAUCE:

2 tbsp (30 mL) olive oil

2 large yellow bell peppers, seeded, finely chopped

1 clove garlic, crushed

1 onion, chopped

1 tbsp (15 mL) paprika

1 tsp (5 mL) crushed red pepper flakes

1 cup (250 mL) chicken broth

1 cup (250 mL) chopped canned plum tomatoes

Salt and freshly ground pepper

FOR THE HASH:

1 1/2 lbs (750 g) new potatoes, scrubbed, quartered

Salt

1/2 lb (250 g) chorizo sausage

1 tbsp (15 mL) olive oil

1 clove garlic, finely chopped

1 onion, finely chopped

1/2 cup (125 mL) oil-packed sun-dried tomatoes, drained (if large, halved)

2 tbsp (30 mL) chopped fresh cilantro

Sprigs fresh cilantro

First, prepare the sauce. Heat the oil in a heavy skillet and sauté the bell peppers, garlic and onion for 5 minutes, or until just beginning to colour. Add the paprika and red pepper flakes and cook for another few minutes. Now, add the broth and tomatoes and season with a little salt and pepper. Bring the mixture to a boil, reduce the heat and simmer for 30 minutes, or until the sauce has thickened. Reduce the heat to as low as possible, cover the sauce and keep warm.

To make the hash, cover the potatoes with boiling water, add a little salt and cook for 5 minutes. Drain the potatoes and set to one side. Place the chorizo on a cutting board and carefully cut it in half lengthwise. Cut each half crosswise into 1-inch (2.5 cm) pieces. Warm the oil in a heavy skillet, add the chorizo and sauté it lightly for about 3 minutes. Add the garlic, onion and sun-dried tomatoes and continue cooking for another minute or so.

Now, add the reserved potatoes and give everything a good mix, continuing to cook until the potatoes are cooked through. Add the chopped cilantro and stir. Remove the hash from the heat. To serve, spoon some of the sauce onto a serving plate and partially cover the sauce with some of the hash. Serve at once with a sprig of fresh cilantro and more sauce if any is left.

 In France, during the time when the potato was just beginning to be accepted, medical opinion was still divided as to its benefits. One doctor maintained that there was "somewhat windy" but "very substantial, good and restorative" nourishment to be had by eating them. Another doctor proclaimed that "boiled, baked or roasted ... eaten with good butter, salt, juice of oranges or lemons and double refined sugar ... they increase seed and provoke lust, causing fruitfulness in both sexes."

Potato & Fresh Sage Gratin

*For this dish you need waxy
potatoes—if possible, those lovely,
long fingerling potatoes. I have also
made this dish, with great success,
using Yukon Golds and red-skinned
potatoes. That's the beauty of potato
dishes—no matter which spuds you
use, they always seem to taste
wonderful. Do make sure you use
fresh sage leaves, though. You could
easily add a bit of precooked
unsmoked bacon, if you wish.*

2 lbs (1 kg) fingerling potatoes or other
    waxy potatoes, scrubbed

4 cloves garlic, thinly sliced

1 1/4 cups (300 mL) heavy cream

Salt and freshly ground pepper

4 tbsp (60 mL) olive oil

20 fresh sage leaves

1/2 cup (125 mL) grated Parmesan cheese

Preheat the oven to 375°F (190°C). Slice the fingerlings lengthwise in half. If
they are larger than usual, slice the potatoes into thirds. (If using more standard
sized potatoes, just thinly slice the whole potato.) In a large bowl, combine the
potato slices with the garlic, cream, salt and pepper, tossing to coat the potato
slices. Use half the olive oil to grease a baking dish and add half the potatoes,
arranged as you wish. Scatter half the sage leaves over the surface, add the
remaining potato slices and pour any accumulated cream over them. Top with
the remaining sage leaves and drizzle the last bit of olive oil over all. Cover with
foil and bake for 45 minutes, removing the foil half way through so that the
potatoes get crusty brown. Sprinkle the cheese over the surface 5 minutes or so
before the end of the cooking time. Remove from the oven and let sit 10 minutes before serving.

Creamed Hash Browns with Wild Mushrooms

3 lbs (1.5 kg) red-skinned potatoes, scrubbed

Salt

3/4 lb (375 g) chanterelles or shiitake
   mushrooms (or an assortment),
   wiped clean

2 tbsp (30 mL) extra virgin olive oil

1/4 lb (125 g) butter

1 large onion, finely chopped

Salt and freshly ground pepper

1 1/4 cups (300 mL) heavy cream

Place the whole potatoes in a large saucepan, cover them with cold water and bring to a boil. Add a little salt and cook until the potatoes are all but cooked through, about 25 to 30 minutes; they should be slightly underdone at the centre. Drain the potatoes, cool, cover with plastic wrap and refrigerate overnight or for at least 6 hours.

Roughly chop the mushrooms. Warm the olive oil in a skillet and sauté the mushrooms for about 5 minutes or so over medium-high heat. Toss them around a bit to get them slightly crispy on the edges, adding a little more olive oil if necessary. Remove the mushrooms from the heat and set them to one side.

Using a paring knife, pull the skins from the potatoes and grate the potatoes on the coarse side of a grater (or in a food processor using the shredding disk). Melt the butter in a large heavy skillet and add the onion. Cook for about 10 minutes and add half the potatoes, a little salt and pepper and the reserved mushrooms. Cover with the remaining potatoes, spreading them evenly and add a little more salt and pepper. Cook, not stirring, until the potatoes start to brown on the bottom, about 6 minutes. Carefully lift up sections of the potato mixture and turn over, repeating until all of it has been turned. Stir the potatoes slightly and pour half the cream over all. After a couple of minutes, stir the potatoes again and add the remaining cream. Cook for another few minutes, or until the potatoes have become nice and crusty and the cream has been absorbed. Serve at once.

This is a luxurious dish, earthy, rich and absolutely bang on with a big, rare steak or prime rib. Use any assortment of mushrooms you like. This dish will taste very good even with good old button mushrooms, but chanterelles and shiitake mushrooms make it really sing. Boil the potatoes the night before you plan to serve them (or early in the same day), refrigerating them until you are ready to use.

Oven-Roasted Potatoes & Parsnips with Curry

MAKES 6 TO 8 SERVINGS

This easy preparation takes the concept of crusty oven-roasted root vegetables one step farther with the addition of a little fragrant curry seasoning. Vary this dish as you wish with turnip, rutabaga, beets, celeriac or carrot. Cut the vegetables in evenly sized pieces and turn them occasionally as they cook to encourage browning and slight caramelizing on as many sides as possible. Vegetables shrink somewhat as they roast in the oven, so you may want to increase the amounts accordingly. Very good with any roasted meats.

5 large baking potatoes, scrubbed
5 large parsnips, peeled
6 large shallots, peeled
1 whole head garlic, cloves separated

1/4 cup (60 mL) extra virgin olive oil
2 tbsp (30 mL) curry powder (or to taste)
Freshly ground pepper

Preheat the oven to 400°F (200°C). Have ready a large roasting pan. Cut the potatoes and parsnips into evenly sized chunks. Place them in a large mixing bowl with the whole shallots and separated (but unpeeled) garlic cloves. Add the olive oil, curry powder and pepper and toss well to coat vegetables. Transfer the vegetables to the pan and roast for about 45 to 60 minutes, tossing and stirring the vegetables around occasionally until they are cooked through and the potatoes and parsnips are crusty and golden brown. Serve hot.

Mash & Mince with Guinness

MAKES 4 TO 6 SERVINGS

FOR THE MINCE:

3 tbsp (45 mL) butter

2 large onions, finely chopped

2 lbs (1 kg) lean ground beef

1 tsp (5 mL) dried rosemary

1 tsp (5 mL) dried thyme

Salt and freshly ground pepper

1 cup (250 mL) Guinness

1 cup (250 mL) rich beef broth

2 tbsp (30 mL) tomato paste

2 tbsp (30 mL) Worcestershire sauce

FOR THE MASH:

2 lbs (1 kg) floury potatoes,
    peeled, quartered

1 tsp (5 mL) salt

1/2 cup (125 mL) butter

3/4 cup (150 mL) whole milk (approx.)

1/2 cup (125 mL) table cream

Melt the butter in a large skillet over medium-high heat. Sauté the onions and the beef together, breaking the beef up as it cooks, for about 10 minutes, or until the beef is browned. Season with the rosemary, thyme, salt and pepper, mixing the seasonings in well. Add the Guinness, broth, tomato paste and Worcestershire sauce and mix together well. Bring to a boil, reduce the heat immediately and simmer for 40 minutes or so, until the mixture has thickened and become sauce-like. If the mixture becomes too thick as it cooks, add a little more broth, Guinness or water and stir to blend.

Meanwhile, prepare the mash. Place the potatoes in a medium-sized saucepan and just cover them with cold water. Bring to a boil, add the salt and cook until the potatoes are tender, about 20 minutes. Drain the potatoes well and shake the pan over low heat for a minute or so to dry the potatoes thoroughly. Mash them with the butter, milk and cream and, finally, whisk to incorporate a little air and make the mash light and fluffy.

Pour a portion of mince in the centre of warmed dinner plates, surround it with the mash and serve.

"Mince and tatties" is a classic Scottish dish that my man-with-Scottish-roots loves. In fact, he enjoyed a big helping of this in a lovely pub in Scotland's little town of North Berwick a few hours before we were married. Certainly the savoury mixture of ground beef and onions, cooked slow and long in a bit of stock and served with mashed spuds, has fed generations of Bravehearts. I've played with the general theme a bit here and also added an Irish influence (my roots!) in the form of Guinness, the stout of champions. Serve with green peas and chunky carrots tossed with butter and parsley.

Angus Potatoes

Inspired by an old-fashioned way of enjoying baked potatoes in Scotland, this is the perfect bit of comfort food to share in front of the fire after a wintry day spent outside. Serve with buttered cabbage, baked tomatoes and good bread.

4 baking potatoes, scrubbed
1 lb (500 g) smoked haddock
1 cup (250 mL) whole milk
1/4 cup (60 mL) heavy cream

3 tbsp (45 mL) whole grain mustard
Freshly ground pepper
1/4 cup (60 mL) chopped fresh
    flat-leaf parsley

Preheat the oven to 400°F (200°C). Place the potatoes directly on the oven rack and bake for about 1 hour. As the potatoes bake, prepare the fish.

Place the smoked haddock in a shallow baking dish, skin side down. Blend the milk, cream and mustard in a little mixing bowl and pour the mixture over the haddock. Season with a little pepper and place the fish in the oven during the last 20 minutes of the potato cooking time. When the fish flakes easily, remove it from the oven.

Remove the potatoes from the oven when they are done and let them cool for a few minutes until you can handle them. Cut a slice from the top of each baked potato and spoon the flesh out into a bowl. Put the hollowed out potato skins and their lids back in the oven to get a little crisp. Mash the potato flesh with the milk and cream used to cook the fish. Add the parsley and blend well into the mashed potatoes. Flake the fish with a fork, discarding any bones or skin.

Preheat the oven broiler. Combine the fish with the mashed potato in the bowl. Place the potato skins and lids on a baking sheet and pile the fish and potato mixture into the skins. Broil the filled skins just to crisp up the surface of the potato filling a bit. Place a crisped potato lid on each potato skin and serve at once.

Honest Clam & New Potato Chowder

MAKES 4 TO 6 SERVINGS

1/4 lb (125 g) unsmoked bacon, finely diced

3 dozen littleneck or cherrystone clams, shucked (about 4 cups/1 L)

2 cups water

1 large white onion, finely diced

1/2 cup (125 mL) oyster crackers (or other unsalted crackers), crushed

1 lb (500 g) new potatoes, scrubbed, diced

3 cups (750 mL) whole milk

1 cup (250 mL) half-and-half cream

Salt and freshly ground pepper

1/4 cup (60 mL) chopped fresh flat-leaf parsley

Place the bacon in a soup pot and sauté over medium-high heat until very crisp. Remove the bacon with a slotted spoon to a paper towel–lined plate. Pour off all but 2 tablespoons (30 mL) of the bacon fat. Place a sieve over a mixing bowl and pour the clams through the sieve, allowing all of the liquid to collect in the bowl beneath. Place the clams in another bowl and rinse them in the water. Now, pour this water through the sieve to combine with the clam liquid. You should have about 3 cups (750 mL) of liquid.

Finely chop the clams, add them to the soup pot along with the onion and sauté in the bacon fat for about 5 minutes. Add the crushed crackers and all of the clam liquid, stir and add the potatoes. Cook over medium heat for about 15 minutes.

As the chowder cooks, heat the milk and half-and-half in a saucepan until hot. Now, add the reserved bits of bacon and the milk and cream mixture to the chowder. Season with a little salt and pepper, sprinkle on the parsley and serve immediately.

You'll need a lot of clams for this, the best white chowder in the universe. Find yourself a good fishmonger, order the clams ahead of time and ask the fishmonger to shuck them and pack them in their own liquid. You'll need 1 cup (250 mL) of the clam liquid for this sumptuous soup. Plan to make it for dinner on Christmas Eve or New Year's Eve. It really is smashing.

There is barely a country or a culture that doesn't celebrate the potato in some form or other. Whether in a myriad of fragrantly spiced dishes in India, comforting *pyrohy* in Ukraine, frites in Belgium, jacket potatoes in the U.K., combined with pasta in Italy or quickly deep-fried in tempura batter in Japan, potatoes are *the* international vegetable. Nowhere is their versatility, compatibility and all-round greatness made more evident than in the thousands of different preparations enjoyed around the world. Here are just a few recipes that give potatoes a new accent every day.

the international potato

Punjabi Potatoes
& Cauliflower

MAKES 4 TO 6 SERVINGS

1 lb (500 g) cauliflower, trimmed

3 large baking potatoes, peeled

1/2 cup (125 mL) vegetable oil

3 onions, finely chopped

2-inch (5 cm) piece fresh gingerroot,
   peeled, slivered

1 tsp (5 mL) coriander

1 tsp (5 mL) salt

1/2 tsp (2 mL) cayenne pepper

1/2 tsp (2 mL) turmeric

1 tsp (5 mL) garam masala

1/2 tsp (2 mL) cumin seeds, roasted, ground

Northern Indian tables often feature potatoes, especially in concert with cauliflower. Here is a typical version that works well as part of an Indian meal or in partnership with roast chicken or pork. Look for the fragrant spice mixture, garam masala, at Indian food shops or other specialty food outlets (or see recipe on page 77). The mixture varies, but generally it includes cardamom, cloves, cumin, cinnamon and nutmeg. Roast the whole cumin seeds in this recipe in a cast-iron pan over medium heat until they are fragrant and begin to turn dark brown. Cool, and then grind them in a coffee grinder or by hand using a mortar and pestle. Serve with Indian-style entrées of chicken or lamb.

Break the cauliflower into florets. Halve the potatoes and cut them into rough chunks. Heat the oil in a wok or large skillet over medium-high heat. When the oil is hot, add the potatoes and quick-fry them for a few minutes, tossing them around until they are just beginning to brown but not cooked through. Transfer them with a slotted spoon to a paper towel–lined plate. Now, do the same with the cauliflower, working in stages, if necessary, frying the cauliflower for just a few minutes until crisp-tender.

Drain off half the oil, return the pan to the heat and sauté the onions until they are beginning to colour and become fragrant, about 5 minutes. Add the gingerroot and stir-fry the mixture for 1 minute. Now, add the coriander, salt, cayenne and turmeric and fry for another minute. Return the potatoes and cauliflower to the pan, mixing well with the onion mixture. Splash in a couple of soup spoonfuls of water, cover the pan, reduce the heat and cook for about 4 minutes, or until the potatoes are tender, adding a little more water if necessary. Remove the pan from the heat and add the garam masala and the ground cumin seeds, stirring them gently into the vegetables. Serve at once.

Spanish Wrinkled Potatoes with Mojo Verde

MAKES 4 TO 6 SERVINGS

FOR THE POTATOES:

3/4 cup (175 mL) sea salt

4 cups (1 L) water

2 1/2 lbs (1.25 kg) small new potatoes, washed

FOR THE MOJO:

4 cloves garlic

1 bunch cilantro, washed, dried, stems removed

1/2 green bell pepper, seeded

1/2 tsp (2 mL) salt

1/4 tsp (1 mL) cumin

3/4 cup (175 mL) extra virgin olive oil

2–3 tbsp (30–45 mL) red or white wine vinegar

Freshly ground pepper

Pour the salt into a large saucepan with the water, stirring to completely dissolve the salt. Add the potatoes (they should be just covered with salt water) and bring to a rapid boil, loosely covered, over high heat. Reduce the heat slightly and boil until potatoes are cooked, about 20 minutes, testing with the tip of a knife to ensure that they are tender all the way through.

Prepare the *mojo* as the potatoes are cooking. Using either a mini food processor or a mortar and pestle, combine the garlic, cilantro, bell pepper, salt and cumin, blending or pounding to form a paste. Gradually add the olive oil, continuing to blend until a thick paste forms. Add the vinegar and some pepper. Scrape the mixture into a little bowl and set to one side.

When the potatoes are cooked, drain off all the water. Keep them in the saucepan and shake the pan occasionally over low heat until the potatoes are dry and the skins slightly wrinkled and coated with a film of dry salt, about 10 to 12 minutes. Serve them immediately with the *mojo*.

Two areas of Spain are renowned for the quality of their potatoes, Galicia in the northwest and the Canary Islands, located hundreds of miles from Spain proper, near the northwestern coast of Africa. It is thought that this way of cooking little new potatoes with coarse salt harks back to a time when, out of necessity, Canary Islanders boiled their potatoes in seawater as fresh water was at a premium. While this may seem like an extraordinary amount of salt, the potatoes are cooked whole and the salt cannot penetrate their skin. The Canary Islands are also famous for their mojos—flavourful, fresh sauces generally based on garlic, herbs, spices, peppers, olive oil and vinegar. Mojo Verde is a fragrant, cilantro-based version. Make sure you use only quality sea salt for this recipe. Wonderful with grilled fish.

Saffron Potato Cakes

Spain naturally comes to mind when we think of saffron, but this potato cake preparation is inspired by little potato cakes I was served by an Italian chef from the north of Italy. A modicum of saffron—the world's most expensive spice—is put to great use in these crispy little cakes with a vibrant golden crust and creamy interior.

3–4 tbsp (45–60 mL) extra virgin olive oil
1 tsp (5 mL) saffron
2 lbs (1 kg) floury potatoes,
   peeled, quartered
Salt

2 large eggs, lightly beaten
2 tbsp (30 mL) chopped fresh
   flat-leaf parsley
1/2 cup (125 mL) all-purpose flour (approx.)
Salt and freshly ground pepper

Place 3 tablespoons (45 mL) of the olive oil in a little dish. Add the saffron and let it soak in the oil while the potatoes cook. Place potatoes in a saucepan, just cover them with cold water, bring to a boil over high heat and add a little salt. Cover loosely and cook until the potatoes are cooked through. Drain and dry thoroughly. Dry mash the potatoes with a masher and transfer them to a mixing bowl. Add the saffron oil, eggs, parsley, a little of the flour and some salt and pepper to the potatoes, blending well to form a dough. At this point, judge whether you need a little more olive oil or flour, depending on how the mixture feels—it should be soft and unsticky. Shape spoonfuls of the mixture into little flattish cakes. Place a skillet over medium heat, add a little of the remaining olive oil and fry until the cakes are golden brown and crispy on both sides, about 6 minutes in total.

Patatas Bravas

2 lbs (1 kg) small waxy potatoes, scrubbed

Salt

4 tbsp (60 mL) olive oil

4 cloves garlic, thinly sliced

1 Spanish onion, finely chopped

1 green bell pepper, seeded, finely chopped

2 dried red chiles, crushed

1 bay leaf, crushed

1 cup (250 mL) canned chopped tomatoes

1/2 cup (125 mL) dry white wine

1 tbsp (15 mL) red wine vinegar

1 tbsp (15 mL) tomato paste

1 tsp (5 mL) hot Spanish paprika

1 tsp (5 mL) sugar

1/2 tsp (2 mL) dried oregano

1/2 tsp (2 mL) dried thyme

Salt and freshly ground pepper

Place the potatoes in a large saucepan, just cover them with boiling water and add a little salt. Bring to a boil over high heat and cook until just tender, 10 to 12 minutes. Drain the potatoes well, let cool for a few minutes, cut them in half and set to one side.

In a large skillet, heat the oil over medium heat and sauté the garlic and onion for a few minutes. Add the bell pepper and continue to cook for about 5 minutes until the vegetables are softened. Add the chiles, bay leaf, tomatoes, wine, vinegar, tomato paste, paprika, sugar, oregano and thyme. Mix the ingredients together well and bring to a gentle boil. Reduce the heat immediately and simmer gently for 10 minutes or so, until the sauce is thickened. Season with a little salt and pepper. Add the potatoes to the sauce and stir to coat them well. Cover and simmer for about 8 minutes more, until the potatoes are tender and cooked through. Serve at once or just warm.

If you have ever enjoyed tapas in Spain, you will be familiar with these spicily sauced potatoes that are often served with additional sauces of mayonnaise or aioli (actually, aïoli, as the Spanish spell it). Adjust the spiciness level here to your tolerance. Look for the hot Spanish paprika at specialty food shops.

Potato Gnocchi with Gorgonzola Cream

Well, by now I guess you've figured out that I really like potato gnocchi because this is the third gnocchi recipe in this book. But they're all quite different from each other and, where these lovely little potato corks are concerned, I don't think you can have too many. This is a classic version, the actual gnocchi consisting of nothing more than potato and flour, with the finished gnocchi combined with a creamy Gorgonzola sauce. These gnocchi, which are also very good with a butter-based tomato sauce, are excellent as a first course before a mild-mannered main dish of veal, chicken or fish. Serve with good, crusty bread so that you can enjoy all the lovely sauce.

FOR THE GNOCCHI:

1 1/2 lbs (750 g) floury potatoes, peeled, quartered

Salt

2 cups (500 mL) all-purpose flour (approx.)

FOR THE CREAM SAUCE:

1/4 cup (60 mL) butter

1/4 lb (125 g) Gorgonzola cheese

2/3 cup (150 mL) heavy cream

Salt and freshly ground pepper

1/2 cup (125 mL) coarsely grated Parmesan cheese

Place the potatoes in a saucepan, just cover them with cold water, bring to a boil, add a little salt and cook until tender, about 20 minutes. Drain well, then peel and dry mash the potatoes until smooth. Transfer them to a work surface lightly dusted with flour. Start to add the flour, a bit at a time, kneading to form a dough; you may not use all the flour. When the dough is soft and smooth, roll it into a long sausage shape, about 3/4 inch (2 cm) in diameter. Cut the roll into pieces about 1-inch (2.5 cm) long, transferring them to a clean tea towel lightly dusted with flour. Don't allow them to touch. Cover with another clean tea towel. Place a large pot of water on to boil.

Now, make the sauce. Melt the butter in a heavy skillet set over medium-high heat. Crumble the Gorgonzola cheese into the butter and stir until it is melted. Add the cream and cook gently over medium-low heat until the sauce is thick. Set to one side.

Add a little salt to the boiling water. Plan to cook the gnocchi in 4 or 5 batches. Using a long-handled strainer or slotted spoon, add the gnocchi to the boiling water; after just a few minutes, they will bob to the surface. Let them cook for just another minute at the surface, remove them with the slotted spoon and transfer them to a lightly buttered, warm serving dish. Repeat with the remaining gnocchi. Make sure that the sauce is still quite warm (if necessary, heat it through gently), pour it over the gnocchi, season with salt and pepper to taste, and scatter the Parmesan cheese over all. Serve at once.

 Chef George Crum is credited with the accidental invention of the potato chip. Crum worked as a chef in Saratoga Springs, New York, during the early 1850s. When an unhappy diner sent back his order of fried potatoes, complaining that they were overly thick, the chef sliced a batch of potatoes as thin as possible, deep-fried them and added a sprinkling of salt. The diner was thrilled and the potato chip—the Saratoga—was born.

Potato, Bean & Corn Empanaditas

MAKES 4 TO 6 SERVINGS

When empanadas, those savoury turnovers made popular by Latin American and Spanish cooks, are made smaller than usual, they become empanaditas, little versions of themselves, and very like Indian samosas, which are also deep-fried. You can deep-fry these if you wish, or try this baked version. Canned or frozen vegetables are fine for the filling. Just make sure to drain them well and, if using frozen vegetables, thaw and drain them. Remove the seeds from the little chile if you don't want too much spice heat.

FOR THE PASTRY:
2 cups (500 mL) all-purpose flour
1/4 tsp (1 mL) salt
1/3 lb (175 g) cold butter
1/3 cup (75 mL) ice water

FOR THE FILLING:
2 medium waxy potatoes, scrubbed, diced
Salt

2 green onions, trimmed, finely chopped
1 small green chile, minced
1/4 cup (60 mL) corn kernels
1/4 cup (60 mL) small lima beans
3 tbsp (45 mL) farmer's cheese (firm, dry cottage cheese), crumbled
1/4 cup (60 mL) chopped fresh cilantro
Salt and freshly ground pepper

Combine the flour and salt in a mixing bowl and cut in the butter in pieces. When the mixture is crumbly, add the ice water and mix to form a dough. Form the dough into 2 disks and wrap them in plastic wrap; let rest for about 30 minutes at room temperature.

Meanwhile, prepare the filling. Place the potatoes in a saucepan, cover them with boiling water, add a little salt and cook for only about 3 minutes. Drain the potatoes well and set to one side. In a mixing bowl, combine the onions, chile, corn, beans, cheese and cilantro and season with salt and pepper. Add the cooled potatoes to this mixture and toss together well.

Preheat the oven to 400°F (200°C). Roll a pastry disk out on a lightly floured surface and cut out rounds about 4-inches (10 cm) wide. Transfer the pastry rounds to a nonstick baking sheet as you work. Place about 1 tablespoon (15 mL) of the filling off-centre on each pastry round. Dip your finger in water and run it around the edge of each round, folding the pastry over to enclose the filling. Seal the edges by pressing them together with the tines of a fork. Repeat the process with the remaining pastry and filling. (If you wish, make the turnovers larger and use more filling for each.) Bake the empanaditas for about 20 minutes until the pastry is golden brown. Serve them while still quite warm or at room temperature.

Initially, people in Italy were quite suspicious of potatoes, and while today the potato is not one of the country's favoured vegetables (as it is in France), it is showcased in a number of special Italian dishes. One of these is from the Abruzzi region where, in the tiny town of San Pio di Fontecchio, *patate sotto il coppo* is made. This potato preparation can be made only during the winter months in houses in which a fire burns constantly. The hearth is cleaned meticulously, then spread with sliced potatoes. A heavy iron lid (the *coppo*) is placed on top and heaped with hot coals. The potatoes are left to cook beneath this searing lid, their fragrance filling the air. Before serving, they are dressed with olive oil and vinegar.

Italian Frico with Potatoes

MAKES 8 SERVINGS

2 tbsp (30 mL) butter

1 large onion, chopped

4 baking potatoes, peeled, thinly sliced

1 1/2 cups (375 mL) beef broth

1 lb (500 g) Montasio cheese, grated

A frico in Italy is a sort of cheese pancake, fried—really fried—until quite firm and very crisp. This version includes thinly sliced potatoes, making it substantial enough to serve as a light supper with a green vegetable and lots of good, crusty bread. A good cheesemonger will have Montasio cheese, a variety without comparison from the Alpine region of Italy known as Friuli.

Melt the butter in a large, preferably nonstick skillet over medium-high heat. Add the onion and sauté for a few minutes. Add the potato slices, turning them over a few times to coat them with the butter and onion. After a minute or so, pour the broth over the potatoes, shaking the pan a little to settle the slices into the broth. Gently cook the potatoes, uncovered, until they are tender and the broth has been completely absorbed.

Now, cover the potatoes with the cheese, spreading it over them evenly. Allow the mixture to cook, browning the cheese around the edges and dotting the surface. You can also slip the skillet under the broiler for a minute or so to brown the frico further. (If much fat is released from the cheese, carefully pour most of it off, leaving a bit behind.) Serve hot.

Sloan's Lamb Stew with Spuds & Stout

MAKES 4 TO 6 SERVINGS

3 lbs (1.5 kg) shoulder lamb chops, bone in

All-purpose flour

3 tbsp (45 mL) bacon drippings or butter

4 onions, quartered

2 cups (500 mL) beef broth

1 cup (250 mL) Murphy's Stout or other
   dark beer

Salt and freshly ground pepper

8 small potatoes, peeled

1 tbsp (15 mL) butter

3 tbsp (45 mL) chopped fresh
   flat-leaf parsley

Trim the chops of any excess fat, pat them dry and dust them very lightly with flour. Melt the drippings or butter in a heavy Dutch oven or similar pot and brown the lamb on all sides in batches. Return all the meat to the pot and add the onions, broth, stout and salt and pepper, lifting the chops so that the liquid flows beneath and over them. Place the peeled potatoes on top of the meat, pressing down to submerge them slightly in the liquid. Cover and gently simmer the stew for about 2 hours, checking from time to time to see that it is not drying out; add a little more broth or water if necessary. When ready to serve, have ready 4 to 6 warmed shallow bowls. Place some of the meat and vegetables in each bowl. Quickly swirl the butter into the remaining meat stock, ladle some over each serving and sprinkle with parsley. Serve at once.

Potatoes and lamb have a natural affinity for each other—certainly the Irish and the Greeks think so. This is my version of an Irish classic and, since my Dad came from the north of Ireland, I don't add carrots to it. In some parts of Ireland, it just isn't an Irish stew without carrots, so if their absence makes you nervous, add them. I don't mind bones in my lamb stew because I think the bonus of more flavour more than makes up for the peskiness of a few bones. All meat is better cooked on the bone, I think. Like most stews, this one is even better the next day, if there are any leftovers. Serve with plenty of white bread and butter.

Pastel de Papas

Pastel is the lovely word for pie and papas is the word for potatoes in Chile, where this beef and potato pie is almost a national way of life. Traditionally, the filling includes quartered hard-boiled eggs, but I prefer my boiled eggs with toast soldiers, so I have omitted them and added a few stuffed green olives to the requisite black ones instead. (Also traditional is the ritualistic little bit of sugar added to the surface of the crust, which you may omit if you wish.)

FOR THE POTATO TOPPING:
3 lbs (1.5 kg) floury potatoes, peeled, cut into chunks
Salt
1/2 cup (125 mL) whole milk
2 tbsp (30 mL) butter
1 tsp (5 mL) nutmeg
Salt and freshly ground pepper

FOR THE MEAT FILLING:
2 tbsp (30 mL) olive oil
2 cloves garlic, finely chopped

2 onions, finely chopped
1 1/2 lbs (750 g) lean ground beef
1/2 cup (125 mL) black seedless raisins, soaked in a little warm water
1/2 cup (125 mL) black olives, pitted
1/2 cup (125 mL) Manzanilla olives, stuffed or pitted
1 heaping tbsp (about 20 mL) paprika
1 tsp (5 mL) cumin
Salt and freshly ground pepper
Sugar (optional)

Prepare the potatoes first. Place them in a large saucepan, cover them with cold water, bring to a boil, add a little salt and cook until the potatoes are tender, about 25 minutes.

While potatoes are cooking, prepare the filling. Warm the olive oil in a large skillet. Add the garlic and onions, frying together for about 6 minutes or so. Now, add the ground beef, breaking it up as it cooks and browns, about 10 minutes. Drain the raisins and add them to the beef, along with the olives, paprika and cumin. Stir all the ingredients together well and season with a little salt and pepper. Cover and remove from the heat.

Drain the potatoes and dry them thoroughly over the heat, shaking the pan back and forth a few times. Mash the potatoes, adding the milk and butter as you work. When the potatoes are well mashed, add the nutmeg, season with a little salt and pepper and, using a wooden spoon, beat the potatoes vigorously until they are smooth and hold their shape.

Preheat the oven to 350°F (180°C). Lightly butter a deep baking dish (like a soufflé dish) and spread a thick (1-inch/2.5 cm) layer of potato on the bottom and up the sides to within 1/2 inch (1 cm) of the top. Carefully transfer the warm meat filling into the centre. Top with the rest of the mashed potatoes, creating a slight dome shape with them. Sprinkle the potatoes with a little sugar, if using. Bake for about 30 minutes, or until the potatoes are golden brown and crusty on the peaks.

 Nineteenth-century philosopher Friedrich (fried rich?!) Nietzsche maintained that "a diet that consists predominantly of rice leads to the use of opium, just as a diet that consists predominantly of potatoes leads to the use of liquor."

Pommes de Terre Lorette

Never heard of Pommes de Terre Lorette, eh? Well, what about tater tots? That is precisely what these delectable gems are and, once you've had the real thing (and they are remarkably easy to make), you'll never buy the supermarket variety again. These little beauties are a combination of puréed potato and pâte à choux (cream puff dough). Worry not; no other pastry is so easy to make.

FOR THE POTATOES:
2 lbs (1 kg) floury potatoes, peeled, quartered
Salt

FOR THE PÂTE À CHOUX:
1 cup (250 mL) water
4 tbsp (60 mL) butter

1/4 tsp (1 mL) salt
Pinch of cayenne pepper
1 cup (250 mL) all-purpose flour
5 eggs
1/2 tsp (2 mL) baking powder
Vegetable oil
1 cup (250 mL) fine, dry breadcrumbs

Place the potatoes in a saucepan, cover them with cold water, bring to a boil and add a little salt. Cook the potatoes until they are quite soft, about 30 minutes. Drain and dry thoroughly by shaking the pan a few times over the heat. Transfer the potatoes to a sieve or strainer and rub them through into a bowl (or use a food mill or potato ricer). Set to one side.

Now, prepare the pâte à choux. Combine the water, butter, salt and cayenne in a heavy saucepan. Bring the mixture to a boil and, when bubbling, add the flour, all at once, beating the mixture until it is smooth and has formed into a ball. Remove from the heat and add the eggs, one at a time, beating well after each addition (use an electric mixer if you wish). Add the baking powder and beat well again.

Heat some vegetable oil in a deep-fryer or similar heavy pot to 375°F (190°C). If you are not using a deep-fryer, use a candy thermometer to gauge the temperature of the oil. Blend the mashed potatoes into the pâte à choux and mix to incorporate well. Moisten your hands slightly and shape the dough into little short logs or small egg shapes, whichever you prefer. Dip them in the breadcrumbs, shaking off the excess. Deep-fry until golden brown on all sides, about 3 minutes in total. Use a slotted spoon to transfer them to a paper towel–lined baking sheet. Serve tots hot!

 Confused about the best potato for your recipe? Round white potatoes are great for frying and for use in gnocchi, gratins and pancakes. The big Idaho-type potatoes are ideal for baking, frying, mashing and using in soups. Choose potatoes from the round red and long white groups for roasting, boiling and using in salads. Older potatoes should be peeled and brought to a boil in cold water; new potatoes can be left unpeeled and cooked in boiling salted water.

Zenia's Potato Pyrohy

My dear friend Zenia Curzon is of Ukrainian heritage and, when she knew I was writing a cookbook devoted to potatoes, she kindly gave me her special recipe for real pyrohy, *also known as* varenyky. *These little plump dumplings are not only filled with potato, but the dough is also made of potato, making them* pyrohy *with a one-two potato punch. Zenia says, "This is a pretty basic recipe for* pyrohy, *but there are probably as many versions as there are Ukrainian moms. My mother does not use mashed potatoes in her dough, but this recipe has always worked really well for me."*

MAKES 4 SERVINGS

FOR THE FILLING:

1 small onion, finely chopped
2 tbsp (30 mL) butter
2 cups (500 mL) warm mashed potatoes
3/4 cup (175 mL) shredded Cheddar cheese
Salt and freshly ground pepper

FOR THE DOUGH:

2 cups (500 mL) all-purpose flour
1 tsp (5 mL) salt
2 egg yolks
1/2 cup (125 mL) cold mashed potatoes
1 tbsp (15 mL) melted butter
1/2 cup (125 mL) cool water (approx.)
Melted butter

Prepare the filling first. Sauté the onion in the butter until softened, about 6 minutes. Combine with the potatoes and cheese and mix well. Season with salt and pepper. Let cool thoroughly before using. (The filling can be made a day ahead and kept covered and refrigerated. Bring to room temperature before using.)

To make the dough, combine the flour and salt in a large mixing bowl. Add the egg yolks, mashed potatoes, melted butter and just enough of the water to form a medium-soft dough. Turn the dough out onto a lightly floured surface and knead until smooth. (Zenia says too much kneading will make the dough tough.) Divide the dough in half and cover with an inverted bowl. Let stand for 10 minutes. Roll out the dough until it is quite thin and cut rounds about 2- to 3-inches (5–8 cm) wide with a large biscuit cutter. Bring a large pot of water to a boil and add a little salt. To each round of dough, add a spoonful of filling and fold over to form a half circle. Press the edges together with your fingers, making sure the *pyrohy* are well sealed. Transfer them to a lightly floured surface and cover them with a clean tea towel so that they do not dry out. Drop a few at a time into the boiling water, stirring gently with a wooden spoon to separate them and keep them from sticking to the bottom of the pot. Boil for 3 to 4 minutes, at which point they should be puffed and bobbing on the surface. (The thinner the dough and the smaller the *pyrohy,* the quicker they will cook.) Transfer with a slotted spoon to a colander, drain thoroughly and place in a warmed bowl. Drizzle with melted butter and toss gently to keep them from sticking together. Cover and keep warm while you cook the remaining *pyrohy*. Serve hot.

Julie's Potato Burritos

MAKES 6 TO 8 SERVINGS

It's debatable, but my good buddy Julie Cohen maintains that she loves potatoes as much as I do. A true fellow potato head, we have shared many a plate of garlic mash, frites, skins and massive bags of Lay's potato chips (plain only, please). Here is Julie's recipe for terrific burritos filled with mashed potato and other good things.

2 lbs (1 kg) floury potatoes, peeled, diced

Salt

2 tbsp (30 mL) olive oil

2 large cloves garlic, minced

1 large onion, finely chopped

1 1/2 tsp (7 mL) chili powder

1 1/2 tsp (7 mL) cumin

6–8 flour tortillas

1/4 lb (125 g) Cheddar cheese, grated

1 jar (7 1/4 oz/215 mL) hot or mild
    taco sauce

Chopped tomatoes and lettuce (optional)

Place the potatoes in a saucepan, cover them with water, bring to a boil, add a little salt and cook them until just tender, about 10 minutes. Drain and cool. In a large skillet, heat the oil over medium heat. Add the garlic and onion and cook until the onion becomes translucent, about 5 minutes. Add the potatoes and cook until golden, about 15 minutes. Add the chili powder and cumin, stirring well to blend. Reduce the heat to low and keep the mixture warm.

Turn another stove element to high and allow it to get very hot. One at a time, move the tortillas quickly over the heat to brown them (alternatively, dry-fry the tortillas in a hot skillet, flipping to lightly brown both sides). Place a tortilla on a plate, top with 1/2 cup (125 mL) of the potato mixture and about 2 tablespoons (30 mL) of the cheese. Add 1 tablespoon (15 mL) of taco sauce and some chopped tomato and lettuce, if desired. Fold up the ends of the tortilla and roll in the sides so that the burrito can be hand held and eaten. Repeat the process with the remaining ingredients.

Pork Souvlaki
with Lemon Potatoes

MAKES 6 SERVINGS

1 1/2 lbs (750 g) boneless pork, cut
    into chunks

4 cloves garlic, minced

Zest of 1 lemon, minced

1/2 cup (125 mL) fresh squeezed
    lemon juice

3 tbsp (45 mL) olive oil

2 tsp (10 mL) paprika

1 1/2 tsp (7 mL) dried oregano

Salt and freshly ground pepper

1 1/2 lbs (750 kg) small red-skinned
    potatoes, scrubbed

Salt

Place the chunks of pork in a large resealable plastic bag (large enough to accommodate the pork and the potatoes). In a small bowl, whisk together the garlic, lemon zest and juice, olive oil, paprika, oregano and salt and pepper. Pour this marinade over the pork, seal the bag and massage the marinade into the meat well. Set to one side.

Place the potatoes in a saucepan, cover them with hot water and bring to a boil. Add a little salt and cook for about 10 minutes, or until just tender. Drain the potatoes and rinse them beneath cold running water until cool. Drain well, pierce the potatoes in a few places with a fork and place them in the bag with the pork, turning the bag over to make sure the marinade coats both the potatoes and the pork. Reseal the bag and refrigerate for at least 2 hours or overnight. (Remove from the refrigerator 30 minutes before cooking.)

Heat the grill to high. Place a colander over a bowl and pour the pork and potatoes into the colander. Divide the pork and potatoes among 6 skewers. Pour the marinade into a small saucepan, bring to a boil, reduce the heat and simmer for a few minutes. Use the marinade to baste the pork and potatoes as they cook on the grill. Reduce the grill heat to medium and grill the skewers for about 15 minutes in total, turning them to brown the meat on all sides. When the potatoes are tender and the meat is just barely pink, remove the skewers from grill. Serve immediately.

Fans of Greek restaurant–style souvlaki and lemony spuds will go for this easy dish in a big way. Make it on a hot summer day accompanied by a classic Greek salad featuring lots of ripe tomatoes, black olives, red onion, feta cheese and cucumber tossed in a herb vinaigrette with romaine. Use wooden skewers (presoaked) so that the meat and potatoes will stay in place while cooking.

Betty's Hotpot

MAKES 4 SERVINGS

4 tbsp (60 mL) butter

1 1/2 lbs (750 g) neck of lamb, cubed

1 large or 2 medium onions, roughly
  chopped

1 tbsp (15 mL) all-purpose flour

1/2–3/4 pint (1 3/4 cups/250–425 mL) light
  stock or hot water

1 tbsp (15 mL) Worcestershire sauce

Salt and freshly ground pepper

1 bay leaf

1 1/2 lbs (750 g) potatoes, peeled,
  thinly sliced

Passionate Coronation Street *fans (like me) will know all about this lamb and spud preparation that has been lauded on television's longest running soap forever. I have made it for more than one fellow fan over the years and, just like the series we revere, it has always been very well rated. This is the "official" recipe, by the way, presented here with the kind permission of* Coronation Street *and Granada Television. If you can't easily obtain neck of lamb, use shoulder or any boneless stewing lamb. (Betty recommends serving with pickled red cabbage or pickled beets.) And I recommend serving it with a cold pint.*

Preheat oven to 325°F (160°C). Melt half of the butter over high heat in a heavy-bottomed frying pan until the fat smokes. Sear the meat and continue frying until nicely browned. Remove the pieces from the pan to a deep casserole or divide among 4 individual high-sided ovenproof dishes.

Turn down the heat to medium. Fry the onions in the pan juices, adding a little more butter if necessary. When the onions are soft and starting to brown, sprinkle on the flour and stir in to soak up the fat and the juices. As the flour paste starts to colour, start adding stock or water a few tablespoons at a time, stirring vigorously to avoid lumps. Gradually add the rest of the liquid. Bring to a simmer, stirring constantly, add the Worcestershire sauce and season with salt and pepper to taste.

Pour the onions and liquid over the meat and mix well. Tuck in the bay leaf (tear into 4 pieces if making individual hotpots).

Taken from the Coronation Street *archive and reproduced courtesy of Granada Media Commercial Ventures.*

Arrange the potatoes over the meat in overlapping layers, seasoning each layer. Dot the top layer of potato with the remainder of the butter.

Cover the dish and place on the top shelf of the oven for 2 hours. Uncover and cook for a further 30 minutes. If the potatoes are not brown by this point, turn up the oven and cook for a further 15 minutes or finish off under the grill, brushing the potato slices with more butter if they look too dry.

 Pommes frites, the French gift to the wonderful world of potato dishes, were long a feature at the French table. But not until the 19th century did a Parisian vendor think of serving them as a snack food in paper cones from his street cart. In no time similar vendors all over Paris were offering hot, crispy frites to residents and tourists alike. When a British tourist took the idea home to England and teamed frites with an already popular street food, fried fish, fish and chips were born.

Raclette with Fingerling Potatoes

MAKES 4 SERVINGS

From Switzerland comes this comfort dish supreme: waxy little new potatoes that are treated to melted cheese and the perfect accompaniment of marinated red onions. It's just the thing after you've spent the day wintering. Raclette cheese, which is rather like Gruyère, may be found marketed as raclette in supermarkets and cheese shops. Italy's Taleggio or fontina cheeses also work well, simply because they melt so beautifully and have the right nutty pungency to accent the mild flavour of the potatoes. Delish served with good bread.

FOR THE MARINATED ONIONS:
2 large red onions, thinly sliced
6 tbsp (90 mL) red wine vinegar
1 1/2 tsp (7 mL) sugar
1/2 tsp (2 mL) salt

FOR THE POTATOES:
1 1/2 lbs (750 g) fingerling potatoes,
    scrubbed (if large, halved)
Salt
Salt and freshly ground pepper
12 oz (375 g) raclette, Gruyère, Taleggio or
    fontina cheese, sliced

Prepare the onions first. Place them in a bowl and just cover them with boiling water. Set to one side. In a little saucepan, blend the vinegar, sugar and salt and heat through, stirring to dissolve the sugar. Remove from the heat and let cool. Drain the onions (now cool), discard the water and combine them with the vinegar mixture, tossing together well. Cover and let sit for a while to let the flavours develop.

Place the potatoes in a saucepan, cover them with boiling water, bring to a boil and add a little salt. Cook the potatoes until just tender, about 15 minutes. Drain and transfer the potatoes to a small roasting pan. Preheat the oven broiler to high. Season the potatoes with a little salt and pepper and arrange the cheese on top. Broil just until the cheese melts, watching to make sure that it doesn't burn. Serve with the marinated onions.

New Potatoes with Thai Flavours

MAKES 4 SERVINGS

1 1/2 lbs (750 g) new potatoes, scrubbed

Salt

1 tbsp (15 mL) vegetable oil

1–2 red Thai chiles, seeded, minced

1 stalk lemon grass, trimmed,
  finely chopped

1 tsp (5 mL) chopped fresh gingerroot

Salt and freshly ground pepper

1/4 cup (60 mL) chopped fresh cilantro

A friend of mine in England sent me this recipe, which she says may not be authentic Thai but works beautifully for any potato heads who love Thai food. This dish is great with satays of chicken or lamb and a little spicy peanut sauce.

Place the potatoes in a saucepan, cover them with boiling water, bring to a boil, add a little salt and cook until tender, about 15 minutes. Drain and cool. Heat the oil in a small saucepan and add the chiles, lemon grass, gingerroot, salt and pepper. Stir-fry for about 5 minutes, or until softened.

Pour this mixture over the potatoes and toss together well. Add the cilantro, toss again and serve.

French Potato
Galette with Bacon

MAKES 6 TO 8 SERVINGS

There are no eggs, cream or milk in this gratin-like preparation of potatoes, bacon and Gruyère cheese. Serve with a lovely green salad and a robust red wine. If you have done as instructed and purchased really good, old-fashioned bacon, it will probably have a rind, so use kitchen shears to neatly trim it away before using the bacon.

2 1/2 lbs (1.25 kg) Yukon Gold
   potatoes, peeled
1 tbsp (15 mL) extra virgin olive oil
1/2 lb (125 g) double-smoked bacon,
   thinly sliced

3/4 lb (375 g) Gruyère cheese, grated
Freshly ground pepper

Place the potatoes in cold water for 15 minutes or so. Drain and pat them dry. Slice the potatoes thinly (use a mandoline if you have one). Soak the potato slices in fresh cold water for another 5 minutes. Pat dry.

Preheat the oven to 425°F (220°C). Oil the bottom and sides of an 9-inch (23 cm) oval or round baking dish. Arrange the slices of bacon on the bottom and sides of the dish, in a spiral fashion, allowing a little more than half the length of each slice to hang over the side.

Cover the bacon in the dish with a third of the potato slices and sprinkle on a third of the cheese. Repeat this procedure with the remaining potatoes and cheese. Cover the tops of the potatoes with the overhanging bacon. (The potatoes should be exposed in the centre.)

Bake for about 1 hour, until the bacon is cooked and the potatoes are tender and golden. Remove the galette from the oven and let sit for 15 minutes. Season with pepper and serve.

Meze Polpettes

MAKES 6 TO 8 SERVINGS

2 lbs (1 kg) floury potatoes,
    peeled, quartered

Salt

1/2 lb (250 g) feta cheese

8 pitted black olives, finely chopped

4 green onions, trimmed, finely chopped

1 large egg, lightly beaten

1/4 cup (60 mL) chopped fresh dill

Juice of 1 lemon

Zest of 1 lemon, minced

Salt and freshly ground pepper

1/2 cup (125 mL) all-purpose flour (approx.)

1/4 cup (60 mL) olive oil

Place the potatoes in a large saucepan, just cover them with cold water, bring to a boil and add a little salt. Cook until the potatoes are tender, about 25 minutes. Drain and dry the potatoes thoroughly over low heat, shaking the pan back and forth a few times. Transfer the potatoes to a mixing bowl and dry mash them. Crumble the feta cheese into the potatoes and add the olives, onions, egg, dill, lemon juice and zest and season with salt (remembering that feta is relatively salty) and pepper. Mix gently with your hands, trying not to break the cheese up too much. Cover with plastic wrap and refrigerate for at least 1 hour (or overnight).

When ready to cook, lightly flour your hands and form the mixture into little balls about the size of a ping-pong ball. Roll them in a little of the flour, shaking off the excess. Transfer the balls to a baking sheet. Heat some of the oil in a heavy pan over medium-high heat. Add a few polpettes to the pan (don't crowd them), flatten them slightly with a metal spatula to form a round patty shape and fry a few minutes until golden brown on both sides, flipping once or twice. Drain on a paper towel–lined plate and keep warm. Serve as soon as all of the polpettes are ready.

Simple to make, these little Greek-style potato patties can be made to form part of a grouping of Mediterranean meze or tapas. Serve them with black olives, marinated grilled calamari, shrimp sautéed with garlic and lemon, dishes of salted, warmed almonds, grilled peppers and something cooling like cucumber in yogurt with fresh dill. Make the mixture the night before if you wish and fry the polpettes just before serving.

Jewish Potato Bread

I think of this wonderful bread with the moist interior and the lovely crusty top as a sort of Jewish focaccia, although you'll find that it is heavier than the Italian bread. (It is rather like a cross between a big latke, or potato pancake, and a savoury kugel, which is a sort of potato or noodle dish.) You can put this together in no time, and it is so easy and fuss free that you'll want to make it often. This bread is absolutely delicious served warm.

MAKES 8 SERVINGS

1/4 cup (60 mL) warm water

1/8 tsp (0.5 mL) sugar

1 tbsp (15 mL) active dry yeast (1 pkg)

2 1/2 lbs (1.25 kg) floury potatoes, peeled

2 1/2 cups (625 mL) unbleached bread flour
   or all-purpose flour

1 tbsp (15 mL) salt

2 tbsp (30 mL) olive oil

2 onions, thinly sliced, sautéed until lightly
   browned

Fill a bowl with hot water and let it sit for a minute. Drain and add the warm water. Dissolve the sugar in the water and add the yeast. Let sit for 10 minutes or so until the yeast is bubbling. As this mixture sits, grate the potatoes using a hand grater or a food processor fitted with the shredding blade. (If a great deal of water comes out of the potatoes, pour most of it off.) Combine the potatoes well with the flour in a large mixing bowl. Add the yeast mixture and the salt and mix well again. Turn the mixture out onto a lightly floured surface, cover with a clean tea towel and wipe the bowl clean. Lightly grease the bowl with a little of the oil and return the dough to it. Cover with the tea towel and leave in a warm place for 50 minutes.

Preheat the oven to 375°F (190°C). Lightly grease a roasting pan or other large baking dish with a little of the oil and cover with the sautéed onions. Distribute the potato mixture over the onions and smooth it out, flattening it somewhat. Bake for 20 minutes, pull out the oven rack and lightly brush the remaining oil over the surface of the bread. Return to the oven and bake until the bread is golden and crusty on the surface.

William Cobbett may not be a household name today, but in the early 1800s he was an outspoken, influential and relatively radical commentator on British life. Among his many dislikes (which included Shakespeare's plays, tea and Parliament) were potatoes. He called potatoes the origin of "slovenliness, filth, misery, and slavery" and described Sir Walter Raleigh, who was reputed to have brought potatoes to England, "one of the greatest villains upon earth." Cobbett claimed that he would rather hang than see Englishmen and women live on the "lazy root."

I am a potato purist. By that I mean that, as much as I love sweet potatoes, I don't consider them really to be potatoes. According to people who study these things, botanically speaking sweet potatoes don't belong to the same family as potatoes. The potato belongs to the Solanaceae family, which includes tomatoes, peppers, eggplant and the deadly nightshade group. The sweet potato belongs to the Convolvulaceae family and apparently is the only member of its clan that is cultivated for human consumption. Sweet potatoes are of two types: one has a rather paler hue than the other, which is moist, full-fleshed and has a deep orange tone. The latter is my choice for these sweet potato recipes—whether they are sweet or savoury preparations. I've also included here a handful of recipes using white potatoes in a sweet capacity. If you have any doubts as to the use of standard white potatoes in this regard, meet the greatest chocolate cake in the universe on page 192!

the sweet potato

Carolina Potato Pie

I once knew a family of Carolinians who moved from the South to New York City many years ago. No doubt because of their Southern roots, these folks always called sweet potatoes "Carolinas." This is the pie they made for every Thanksgiving— and I think it is the best sweet potato pie I have ever tasted. Serve it with unsweetened whipped cream.

FOR THE PASTRY SHELL:
2 cups (500 mL) all-purpose flour
1/4 tsp (1 mL) salt
1/3 lb (175 g) unsalted butter
1/3 cup (75 mL) ice water

FOR THE FILLING:
2 lbs (1 kg) sweet potatoes, peeled
1 cup (250 mL) dark brown sugar, packed
3 tbsp (45 mL) white sugar

1/4 lb (125 g) butter, softened
1 tsp (5 mL) cinnamon
1/4 tsp (1 mL) ginger
1/4 tsp (1 mL) nutmeg
1/2 tsp (2 mL) salt
3 large eggs, separated
1/2 cup (125 mL) freshly squeezed
 orange juice
1/2 cup (125 mL) table cream
Zest of 1 small orange, finely chopped

First, prepare the pastry. Combine the flour and salt in a mixing bowl and cut in the butter in pieces. When the mixture is crumbly, add the ice water and mix to form a dough. Wrap the dough in plastic wrap and chill for about 1 hour. Roll the dough out on a lightly floured surface and cut to fit a 9-inch (23 cm) pie pan. Line the pan with the pastry and set to one side.

Preheat the oven to 425°F (220°C) and prepare the filling. Place the sweet potatoes in a large saucepan, cover them with cold water, bring to a boil and cook, loosely covered, over medium heat until soft, 15 to 20 minutes. Drain well and transfer the sweet potatoes to a large mixing bowl. Let cool for a minute or so and then mash the sweet potatoes, adding both sugars and the butter, cinnamon, ginger, nutmeg and salt. Beat this mixture to blend well. In a separate bowl, whisk the egg yolks together for a few minutes. Add them to the sweet potato mixture, along with the orange juice, cream and orange zest, beating the mixtures to blend them well. In a dry mixing bowl, beat the egg whites until stiff, using a hand-held blender or electric mixer. Gently fold the egg whites into the sweet potato mixture. Place the mixture in the pastry shell, gently smoothing the top. Bake for about 12 minutes, reduce the temperature to 350°F (180°C) and bake about another 30 minutes or so, until the pie filling is puffed up and a tester inserted in the centre of the pie comes out clean. Remove the pie from the oven and let cool before serving.

 I Yam What I Yam. Confused about yams and sweet potatoes? Well, who wouldn't be, since they are often even mislabelled at grocery outlets! Sweet potatoes come in a number of varieties, but generally your supermarket will stock either a pale or a dark variety. It is the darker variety that many of us call yams. This variety has a thicker, orange skin and quite bright orange, sweet, moist flesh. The pale sweet potatoes have a thin, light yellow skin and similarly coloured flesh that is not particularly sweet. True yams, on the other hand, are from an entirely different family of plants and come in many varieties, large and small, and have rather shaggy brownish exteriors. Their flesh may range in colour from off-white to a rather pale yellow and their texture can run from moist to mealy.

Sweet Potato Soufflé

This light-as-air soufflé is just as nice at the beginning of a meal as it is at the end, being sort of a cross between a savoury and a sweet concoction. If you want to maximize the savoury side, omit the sugar, cinnamon and nutmeg and add a little full-flavoured grated cheese.

MAKES 6 SERVINGS

3 large sweet potatoes, unpeeled

3 extra large eggs, separated

1/4 cup (60 mL) sugar

3 tbsp (45 mL) butter

2 tbsp (30 mL) whole milk

1/4 tsp (1 mL) cinnamon

1/4 tsp (1 mL) nutmeg

Pinch of salt

Preheat the oven to 400°F (200°C). Lightly butter a 6-cup (1.5 L) soufflé dish. Place the whole sweet potatoes in a large saucepan, cover them with cold water and bring to a boil. Cook until the sweet potatoes are tender, about 25 minutes. Drain and leave them until cool enough to handle. When cool, peel the sweet potatoes and mash them with the egg yolks, 1 tablespoon (15 mL) of the sugar, 2 tablespoons (30 mL) of the butter and the milk, cinnamon, nutmeg and salt. Mix well.

In another bowl, whisk the egg whites using a hand-held blender or electric beater, until stiff peaks form. Gently fold the egg whites into the sweet potato mixture. Carefully pour this mixture into the soufflé dish, dot the surface with the remaining butter and sprinkle with the remaining sugar. Bake for about 30 minutes until puffed and golden brown. Serve immediately.

Sweet Potato Pancakes with Maple Butter

MAKES 4 TO 6 SERVINGS

1 cup (250 mL) all-purpose flour

1 tbsp (15 mL) light brown sugar

1 tsp (5 mL) baking powder

1/2 tsp (2 mL) baking soda

1/2 tsp (2 mL) cinnamon

1/2 tsp (2 mL) nutmeg

1/4 tsp (1 mL) salt

1 large egg, beaten

3/4 cup (175 mL) mashed sweet potatoes

3/4 cup (175 mL) whole milk

1/2 cup (125 mL) plain yogurt

2 tbsp (30 mL) butter, melted

Vegetable oil

In a mixing bowl, combine the flour, sugar, baking powder, baking soda, cinnamon, nutmeg and salt, stirring to blend. In another bowl, combine the egg, mashed sweet potato, milk, yogurt and melted butter. Add the dry ingredients to the sweet potato mixture, gently folding in to blend but being careful not to over-mix.

Warm the oven. Place a cast-iron pan or griddle on high heat. When the pan is quite hot, add a little vegetable oil, swirl it around to coat and add 1/4 cup (60 mL) of the batter per pancake. When little bubbles appear on the surface of the pancake, flip it and cook the other side until browned. Transfer to a plate and keep warm in the oven as you make the rest of the pancakes. Serve immediately with maple butter.

Sweet potatoes are a natural as far as pancake-making is concerned. They lend lightness and a lovely element of sweetness to the batter and are outstanding with the usual accoutrements of smoky bacon or sausages. Maple butter is an all-Canadian product that you should be able to find wherever quality maple syrup is produced. It has the consistency of thick honey and is just the thing for these pancakes. If you can't find it, use apple butter or homemade apple sauce sweetened with pure maple syrup.

Sweet Potato–Crusted Shrimp

MAKES 6 TO 8 SERVINGS

Make these shrimp as a special hors d'oeuvre—they are crispy, colourful and very pretty. They have a nice balance of sweet to spicy and go very well with a dry bubbly. You can prepare them ahead of time if you wish as they are quite good when reheated in a hot oven.

6 green onions, trimmed, finely chopped

3 cloves garlic, minced

2 lbs (1 kg) sweet potatoes, peeled, finely grated

3/4 cup (175 mL) chopped fresh cilantro

1/4 cup (60 mL) light soy sauce (light, as in light-coloured)

2 tbsp (30 mL) fresh gingerroot, minced

1 tsp (5 mL) curry powder

1 tsp (5 mL) sesame oil

Salt and freshly ground pepper

1 1/4 cups (300 mL) all-purpose flour (approx.)

1 lb (500 g) uncooked large shrimp, peeled, deveined (frozen shrimp are fine)

Vegetable oil

In a large bowl, combine the green onions, garlic, sweet potato, cilantro, soy sauce, gingerroot, curry powder, sesame oil, salt and pepper. Blend well and add 1 cup (250 mL) of the flour.

Pat the shrimp dry and lightly dredge them in the remaining flour, shaking off the excess. Place the shrimp a few at a time in the sweet potato mixture and pat the mixture onto the shrimp, coating them well. Transfer the shrimp to a baking sheet and repeat with the remaining shrimp. Heat 3 inches (8 cm) of oil to 350°F (180°C) in a heavy skillet, using a candy thermometer to gauge the temperature. Carefully place the shrimp in the hot oil, just a few at a time, and cook briefly for about 2 minutes in total, turning once. Transfer the cooked shrimp to a paper towel–lined plate to drain. (If reheating, place the shrimp in a 400°F/200°C oven for about 5 minutes.)

Sweet Potato
Hush Puppies

MAKES 4 TO 6 SERVINGS

1 cup (250 mL) mashed sweet potatoes

1 onion, finely chopped

3 eggs

1/2 cup (125 mL) cornmeal

1/2 cup (125 mL) unbleached bread flour
   or all-purpose flour

1/2 tsp (2 mL) salt

1/4 tsp (1 mL) cayenne pepper

Freshly ground pepper

Lard or oil

Combine the sweet potatoes with the onion in a mixing bowl and add the eggs, one at a time, beating after each addition. Add the cornmeal, flour, salt, cayenne and pepper and blend well. Heat a little lard or oil in a cast-iron skillet over medium-high heat. Drop spoonfuls of the sweet potato mixture into the skillet and fry for about 5 to 6 minutes, turning the hush puppies to brown them evenly on both sides. Add a little more lard or oil to the pan for each batch and allow it to get hot before frying the remaining hush puppies. Serve hot.

In the southern U.S., the little savoury fritters known as hush puppies are always served at outdoor fish fries. I love these "pups" (as Southerners refer to them) with good ham, fried chicken, collard greens and rice. While they are usually deep-fried, this version featuring mashed sweet potatoes may be pan-fried or deep-fried. Lard is the traditional cooking fat, but you may use olive or other vegetable oil if you prefer.

Bittersweet Chocolate Potato Cake with Chocolate Orange Icing

MAKES 8 TO 10 SERVINGS

It's amazing what a little potato can do to improve the average chocolate cake. Not that this fab example could possibly be considered average. This cake has a wonderful deep, dark chocolate flavour and an unfailingly moist texture, thanks to our friend the tuber. This is the perfect special day cake. My Mum always added fresh squeezed orange juice to her dark chocolate icing, so I do, too. Serve this cake with unsweetened whipped cream.

FOR THE CAKE:
1/2 cup (125 mL) unsweetened best
   quality cocoa
2 tbsp (30 mL) boiling water
4 squares (4 oz/125 g) unsweetened
   chocolate, chopped
3/4 cup (175 mL) whole milk
1 cup (250 mL) butter, softened
2 cups (500 mL) sugar
4 large eggs, separated
2 tsp (10 mL) pure vanilla extract
1 cup (250 mL) dry mashed potatoes

2 cups (500 mL) all-purpose flour
1 tsp (5 mL) baking powder
1 tsp (5 mL) baking soda
1 tsp (5 mL) salt

FOR THE ICING:
5 squares (5 oz/155 g) unsweetened
   chocolate, chopped
1 cup (250 mL) unsalted butter
3 1/2 cups (875 mL) sifted icing sugar
Juice of 1 large orange
Pinch of salt

Preheat the oven to 375°F (190°C). Lightly butter and flour two 8-inch (20 cm) cake pans and set to one side. Place the cocoa in a small bowl and whisk in the boiling water to form a paste. Set to one side. Place the 4 chocolate squares and milk in a small saucepan and heat over medium heat, stirring to melt the chocolate and incorporate it into the milk. Remove the mixture from the heat and whisk in the reserved cocoa paste. Set to one side.

Using an electric mixer or regular hand mixer, cream the butter and sugar together. While still mixing, add the egg yolks one at a time, beating well after each addition. Add the vanilla, keep mixing, and then gradually add the reserved chocolate mixture. Pass the mashed potato through a sieve into the chocolate mixture and stir the mixtures together well.

Combine the flour, baking powder, baking soda and salt in another bowl, blending together with a fork or whisk. Slowly add the dry ingredients to the chocolate mixture and blend together; do not overmix. Set the batter to one side.

In another bowl, beat the egg whites until peaks form. Using a rubber spatula, combine the egg whites with the chocolate batter, folding the two together gently. Pour the batter into the prepared cake pans and place them in the centre of the oven. Bake for about 50 minutes, or until a tester inserted in the centre of the cakes comes out clean.

Remove the cakes from the oven and cool in the pan for about 15 minutes. Turn them out onto a baking rack and let cool while you prepare the icing.

Melt the 5 chocolate squares by placing them in a small bowl set over a saucepan of very hot water. Stir with a wooden spoon until the chocolate is melted. Remove from the heat and let cool.

Using an electric mixer, beat the butter until light and fluffy. Gradually add the icing sugar and continue beating the mixture. When all of the icing sugar has been incorporated, add the melted chocolate, scraping it into the sugar mixture with a spatula, followed by the orange juice and salt. Stir the icing well until it is smooth and creamy. Transfer a cake layer to a platter, spread a portion of the icing over the top of the layer, smoothing the icing to the edges. Top with second cake layer and ice the top and sides of the whole cake.

Sweet Potato Dumplings with Blackberries & Cream

MAKES 6 TO 8 SERVINGS

On the Richter scale of desserts, this one buries the needle. Very Southern, very old-fashioned and one of the best things to do with sweet potatoes—ever. Don't restrict yourself to blackberries for this dish. Any ripe fruit in season—berries, peaches, pears, apples, plums—can be slow-cooked and served alongside. You don't require a great deal of sweet potato for this recipe, so choose a small one. I urge you to serve unsweetened, softly whipped cream with the dumplings and fruit sauce. Plan a light main course if you're going to have these for dessert.

FOR THE BLACKBERRIES:

4 cups (1 L) blackberries (or a combination of berries or other fruit)

2 cups (500 mL) water

3/4 cup (175 mL) sugar (this amount is approximate, depending on the sweetness of the fruit)

1 tbsp (15 mL) fresh lemon juice (or to taste)

FOR THE DUMPLINGS:

1 1/4 cups (300 mL) all-purpose flour

2 tsp (10 mL) baking powder

1 tsp (5 mL) sugar

1/2 tsp (2 mL) salt

1 cup (250 mL) whole milk

Scant 1/2 cup (125 mL) mashed sweet potatoes

2 tbsp (30 mL) butter, melted

First, prepare the fruit. Combine the blackberries or other fruit with the water and sugar in a heavy-based saucepan. Bring to a rapid boil, reduce the heat and simmer until the fruit is softened, about 5 minutes or so, being careful not to overcook. Add a little lemon juice, stir it in and then taste the fruit. If it is too sweet, add a little more lemon juice. (Other flavourings can also be added, such as liqueurs or port, depending on the fruit.) Set the fruit sauce to one side while you prepare the dumplings.

Combine the flour, baking powder, sugar and salt in a large mixing bowl, blending well. In another bowl, beat together the milk and mashed sweet potato until smooth. Add the melted butter, beating it in quickly. Now, add the sweet potato mixture all at once to the dry ingredients, working the mixtures together lightly; do not overmix.

Return the saucepan containing the sauce to low heat. When the sauce is simmering again, drop heaping tablespoonfuls of the sweet potato batter into it, using the spoon to shape the batter into a dumpling shape. Repeat with the remaining batter, pushing the dumplings gently down into the sauce to cook. Cover and let cook gently for about 5 minutes, longer if you have made larger dumplings. Spoon some sauce into shallow bowls, top with dumplings and spoon some more sauce over them. Pass the cream!

 One of the reasons for the early distrust of the potato plant was the way it reproduced. In the 1600s, botanists and the general public alike were used to edible plants reproducing from seeds, not tubers, as was the case with the potato. When the Swiss botanist Gaspard Bauhin stated that the potato belonged to the *Solanum* genus—the same genus as deadly nightshade, tobacco and the tomato, eggplant and sweet pepper, all of which had very negative connotations at the time—he furthered the belief that the potato was poisonous or narcotic.

Potato Marzipan

2 cups (500 mL) blanched almonds
1/4 cup (60 mL) prepared instant
 mashed potatoes (or regular, dry
 mashed potatoes)
4 cups (1 L) icing sugar

1 egg white, lightly beaten
1/4 tsp (1 mL) almond extract
Cornstarch
Food colouring

Ordinarily I am not a fan of "instant" potatoes; preferring the real thing in all things is pretty much my credo. However, this is a pretty handy little preparation that will enable you to make something that is very like authentic (and sometimes pricey) almond marzipan. It uses some of those instant spuds (although you can also use the same amount of homemade dry mashed potato) and, once they are combined with the other ingredients, they seem to make the resulting mixture very pliable and easy to work with. Kids love to model this edible dough and make no end of sweet little fruits, vegetables, animals, figures or other shapes. Once made, the shapes can be painted with food colouring and other cookie decorating ingredients. Get the kids to lightly dust their hands with cornstarch before shaping the dough.

Place the almonds in a blender or food processor and process until they are ground to a fine powder. Combine the almonds, mashed potatoes and icing sugar in a large mixing bowl. In another bowl, whisk together the egg white and the almond extract. Now, add the egg white mixture, a little at a time, to the potato mixture. You want to add just enough to make the dough pliable. Form the dough into a ball, cover with plastic wrap and refrigerate for 30 minutes.

Lightly dust your hands with cornstarch before working with the dough. Break off a little of the dough and start experimenting! Make little shapes and paint them with food colouring or dip them in melted chocolate. Allow them to dry thoroughly on a rack before storing them in an airtight container. Serve these marzipan treats as part of a sweets offering after dinner or use them as decorations.

Irish Potato Apple Griddle Cake

MAKES 4 TO 6 SERVINGS

1 cup (250 mL) all-purpose flour (approx.)

1/4 cup (60 mL) chilled butter (approx.)

1/2 tsp (2 mL) baking powder

1/2 tsp (2 mL) salt

3 cups (750 mL) dry mashed potatoes

2 large apples, peeled, cored (Spys are a
   good choice)

1 tbsp (15 mL) sugar (approx.)

1 tsp (5 mL) cinnamon

1/4 tsp (1 mL) cloves

2 tbsp (30 mL) butter (approx.)

Combine the flour and butter in a mixing bowl. Work the butter into the flour, as for making pastry. When the mixture is crumbly, add the baking powder and salt and mix in well. Now, add the mashed potatoes and use your hands to blend the ingredients, forming a dough. Turn the dough out onto a lightly floured surface and knead lightly for a few minutes, working in a bit more flour if the dough is sticky. Divide the dough into 2 balls. Roll each one out about 1/2-inch (1 cm) thick. Cover them with a clean tea towel.

Slice the apples thinly directly over a bowl. Add the sugar, cinnamon and cloves and toss the apple slices to coat them. Uncover the dough and layer the apple slices on one of the circles. Dot with some of the butter and cover with the other dough circle, pinching the edges to seal in the filling.

Heat a griddle or cast-iron pan over medium-high heat and add a little butter, brushing it over the surface as it melts. Carefully transfer the cake to the pan, reduce the heat to low and slowly fry the potato cake until speckled golden brown on both sides, about 15 to 20 minutes. Serve hot.

This preparation has much tradition behind it. In the Celtic year, October 31 is a very significant date. It is All Saints' Day, essentially New Year's Eve, because—according to the Celtic calendar—the Celtic year starts on November 1, and so begins the ancient Celtic festival Samhain. A number of sacred foods are included in the celebration, among them apples and potatoes. Here is an ancient recipe that combines both these foods while providing delicious comfort. Serve hot with a wee bit of thick cream, if desired, and cups of hot, strong tea.

Pratie Oaten

MAKES 4 SERVINGS

Now, this is not really a dessert recipe in the strict sense, but since I love cheese with oat crackers in place of a sweet at the close of a good meal, I have decided to include this recipe here. Actually, pratie (the Irish word for potatoes) oaten are traditional little breakfast griddle breads, served with eggs, black pudding, sausage and the like. But, I have discovered that if you roll them thinner and let them cool, they make wonderful accompaniments to good cheese, especially, ahem, Scottish Cheddar (for my husband) and Irish Cashel blue (for me). Try them, too, spread with lemon curd or homemade jams.

2 cups (250 mL) warm, dry mashed potatoes
1/2 cup (125 mL) all-purpose flour
1 cup (250 mL) uncooked oatmeal

1/2 tsp (2 mL) salt
1/2 cup (125 mL) butter, melted

In a mixing bowl, combine the mashed potatoes with the flour, all but 1 tablespoon (15 mL) of the oatmeal and the salt. Using your hands, work the mixture together to form a soft dough. Add the melted butter to the dough and blend it in. (If the dough seems too sticky or too dry, add a little more flour or butter as required.)

Preheat the oven to 375°F (190°C). Scatter the remaining oatmeal on a dry surface and roll out the dough about 1/4-inch (5 mm) thick (or as thin as you can). Using a biscuit cutter, cut out rounds of the dough and transfer them to a baking sheet covered with parchment paper. Bake for about 20 minutes, checking now and then to see that they are not browning too quickly, until crisp and lightly browned. Let cool on the baking sheet for a few minutes before transferring them to a cooling rack with a metal spatula. Let cool before serving.

Buttermilk Biscuits with Sweet Potato

MAKES 4 TO 6 SERVINGS

2 cups (500 mL) all-purpose flour	1/2 tsp (2 mL) salt
3 1/4 tsp (16 mL) baking powder	5 tbsp (75 mL) butter or shortening, chilled
1 tsp (5 mL) sugar	3/4 cup + 2 tbsp (205 mL) buttermilk
1/2 tsp (2 mL) baking soda	1/2 cup (125 mL) mashed sweet potatoes

Preheat the oven to 500°F (260°C). Sift the flour, baking powder, sugar, baking soda and salt together into a mixing bowl. Add the butter or shortening (make sure it is chilled) and work it into the dry ingredients with your fingers, as for making pastry. Add the buttermilk and sweet potato and, working quickly, stir the mixture together with a wooden spoon; don't work past the point at which the mixture turns into a dough. Turn the dough out onto a lightly floured surface and pat it—don't roll it—out 3/4-inch (2 cm) thick to about an 8-inch (20 cm) square. Use a biscuit cutter to cut the dough into 2-inch (5 cm) rounds. Place them on an ungreased baking sheet and bake for just 8 minutes, or until lightly browned.

Try these the next time you make fried chicken—okay, the next time you bring fried chicken home (wink, wink) or with absolutely any chicken at all. These biscuits go into a very hot oven for just a few minutes, so watch them carefully. Serve them hot with plenty of butter.

Grand Sweet Potato Cheesecake with Pecan Crust

SERVES A CROWD (UP TO 20 PEOPLE)

This is a serious cheesecake, one that you should plan to make when you have enough people on hand to do it justice. It depends on the crowd, of course, but I think you could serve almost 20 people with it, owing to the fact that it is big and rich. Make this cheesecake for Thanksgiving or Christmas or as the conclusion to any special cold-weather dinner. Yes, I know this is a lot of cream cheese, but that's what a real cheesecake calls for. Besides, you don't make a cake like this every day. You will need a 10-inch (25 cm) springform pan for this cheesecake, which you should make the day before you plan to serve it.

FOR THE CRUST:

1 1/2 cups (375 mL) finely chopped pecans

2 tbsp (30 mL) butter, softened

2 tbsp (30 mL) sugar

FOR THE FILLING:

4 large eggs, lightly beaten

3 egg yolks, lightly beaten

2 1/2 lbs (1.25 kg) cream cheese

1 cup (250 mL) sugar

3 tbsp (45 mL) all-purpose flour

2 tsp (10 mL) cinnamon

1 tsp (5 mL) ginger

1 tsp (5 mL) nutmeg

2 cups (500 mL) mashed sweet potatoes

1 cup (250 mL) heavy cream

1 tbsp (15 mL) pure vanilla extract

First, prepare the crust. Preheat the oven to 400°F (200°C). Combine the pecans, butter and sugar in a mixing bowl and blend together thoroughly. Press this mixture into the bottom and a third of the way up the sides of a 10-inch (25 cm) springform pan. Bake for just 6 minutes, or until the crust is beginning to brown. Watch carefully and don't allow the crust to overbake. Remove the crust from the oven and allow to cool before using. Leave the oven on.

Now, prepare the filling. Combine, by hand or by using an electric mixer, the eggs and yolks, cream cheese and sugar, blending well until the mixture is creamy. Add the flour, cinnamon, ginger and nutmeg and continue to blend. Now, add the sweet potato, cream and vanilla and continue to beat until all of the ingredients are mixed together well. Pour this mixture into the prepared, cooled crust and bake for 15 minutes. Reduce the temperature to 275°F (140°C) and bake the cheesecake for another hour.

At this point, turn off the heat completely, but leave the cake in the oven overnight to complete baking in the residual heat and eventually to cool. In the morning, loosely cover the cheesecake with plastic wrap or waxed paper and refrigerate, if you wish to serve chilled. When serving, have ready a sharp knife and a measuring cup of boiling water. Dip the knife in the water and slice the cheesecake once; wipe the knife clean and dip in the water before slicing the cheesecake again.

While potatoes do not have aphrodisiac qualities, as was once believed, they certainly were instrumental in helping to increase the population of Ireland. By the middle of the 18th century, potatoes were the mainstay of the Irish diet, enabling families to thrive. The population of Ireland grew from just over 3 million in 1755 to more than 8 million in 1845, a figure that was to drop dramatically shortly after with the advent of the potato blight and the Great Famine.

Potato & Almond Cake

Again, here is the cake to make when you have some leftover mashed potato. If you don't, you can quickly microwave a big baking potato until soft, mash it and then proceed with the recipe. While this cake may sink a little in the centre after cooling, the bonus is that it stays moist long after other cakes become dry. Very good with your 11 a.m. coffee. You will need a 9-inch (23 cm) springform pan for this cake.

MAKES 8 TO 10 SERVINGS

1 cup (250 mL) whole, unskinned almonds
1 cup (250 mL) golden raisins
2 tsp (10 mL) baking powder
3 eggs, separated
3/4 cup (175 mL) sugar

1/4 cup (60 mL) butter, softened
2 tbsp (30 mL) brandy
1 cup (250 mL) cold mashed potatoes
Icing sugar

Preheat the oven to 350°F (180°C). Lightly butter the bottom and sides of the pan. Cut out a circle of parchment paper to fit the bottom of the pan and lightly butter the paper, too. Grind the almonds to a powder, either in a blender, coffee grinder or food processor. Combine the ground almonds with the raisins and baking powder in a small bowl and set to one side. Beat the egg whites in another bowl until they thicken and start to form soft peaks. Add half of the sugar and continue to beat until the egg whites are stiff and glossy.

In a large bowl, combine the remaining sugar with the butter until the mixture is light and creamy. Whisk in the egg yolks and brandy. Gently fold in the mashed potatoes, almond mixture and egg whites. Carefully transfer the batter to the prepared pan, smooth the surface of the batter gently and bake for 30 to 40 minutes, or until a tester inserted in the centre of the cake comes out clean. Let the cake cool in the pan on a rack for 15 minutes before removing the frame of the springform pan. Set the cake on a platter and dust with icing sugar. Serve warm or at room temperature.

Sweet Potato, Apple & Sausage Stuffing

MAKES ABOUT 7 CUPS (1.75 L) (PERFECT FOR A 10 LB/4.5 KG TURKEY)

3 tbsp (45 mL) butter

2 stalks celery, trimmed, finely chopped

1 onion, finely chopped

1 apple, peeled, cored, finely chopped

4 cups (1 L) mashed sweet potatoes

2 cups (500 mL) dry breadcrumbs

3 tbsp (45 mL) chopped fresh
   flat-leaf parsley

1 tbsp (15 mL) dried sage

1 tbsp (15 mL) dried thyme

Salt and freshly ground pepper

1 egg, lightly beaten

1/2 lb (250 g) sausage meat

This terrific stuffing combines sweet potato with sausage and other traditional stuffing ingredients. Now, you'll never again have to wonder how you're going to fit the sweet potatoes in the oven at the same time as the turkey.

In a large skillet, melt the butter and sauté the celery and onion for a few minutes until softened. Let cool. Combine the celery mixture in a mixing bowl with the apple, sweet potatoes, breadcrumbs, parsley, sage and thyme and season with salt and pepper. Mix in the egg and sausage meat, using your hands to combine the ingredients well. If the stuffing seems too wet, add another 1/2 cup (125 mL) or so of breadcrumbs; if too dry, add a little orange juice. Let the stuffing cool completely before using it to stuff a turkey or chicken. Any extra stuffing can be baked alongside the bird in a lightly greased pan.

Sweet Potato Pound Cake with Sweet Potato Ice Cream

MAKES 8 SERVINGS

A double hit of sweet potato sweets, this is a beautifully coloured, flavourful cake with a great, densely crumbed texture, thanks to the nuts. The sweet potato ice cream does require an ice cream machine; if you don't own one, just make the cake, buy some good quality vanilla or rum and raisin ice cream to serve alongside and ask for an ice cream machine for your birthday. You will need a total of 2 cups (500 mL) mashed sweet potatoes to make both preparations, about 2 to 3 sweet potatoes, depending on their size.

FOR THE ICE CREAM:

8 large egg yolks

1 cup + 2 tbsp (280 mL) sugar

1/4 tsp (1 mL) salt

2 1/4 cups (550 mL) heavy cream

2 1/4 cups (550 mL) whole milk

1 1/2 cups (375 mL) mashed sweet potato

1 tsp (5 mL) cinnamon

1/2 tsp (2 mL) ginger

1/2 tsp (2 mL) nutmeg

FOR THE CAKE:

1 1/2 cups (375 mL) cake flour

1/2 tsp (2 mL) baking soda

1/2 tsp (2 mL) cinnamon

1/2 tsp (2 mL) nutmeg

1/2 tsp (2 mL) salt

1/2 cup (125 mL) butter, softened

1 cup + 6 tbsp (340 mL) sugar

1/2 cup (125 mL) buttermilk

3 large eggs, lightly beaten

1/2 cup (125 mL) mashed sweet potatoes

1/2 cup (125 mL) pecans, lightly toasted (skillet or oven), chopped

1 tsp (5 mL) pure vanilla extract

Combine the egg yolks, sugar and salt in a large bowl and whisk together until smooth. Set to one side. Combine the cream and milk in a heavy-based saucepan and bring to a boil over medium heat. Remove from the heat and slowly add the milk mixture to the egg yolks, whisking all the while. Place this mixture in the refrigerator and leave to get quite cold (start working on the cake at this point). When the mixture is quite cold, strain it through a sieve and combine it with the sweet potatoes, cinnamon, ginger and nutmeg. Freeze this mixture according to your ice cream maker's instructions.

Preheat the oven to 300°F (150°C) and prepare the cake. Lightly butter a 9- × 5-inch (2L) loaf pan. Into a large mixing bowl, sift together the flour, baking soda, cinnamon, nutmeg and salt. Set to one side. In another bowl, cream together the butter and sugar until smooth. Add the buttermilk and blend into the flour mixture. Stir in the eggs, sweet potato, pecans and vanilla, incorporating all ingredients. Fold the dry ingredients into the batter in one or two stages, mixing just until blended and no traces of flour remain. Pour into the prepared pan and bake for 40 to 50 minutes, or until a tester inserted in the centre of the cake comes out clean. Let the cake cool in the pan on a rack for 15 minutes, and then turn the cake out of the pan to cool completely.

 In Shakespeare's *Merry Wives of Windsor,* Falstaff, who thinks he is about to enjoy the pleasures of two women at once, says to one of them: "Let the sky rain [sweet] potatoes ... let there come a tempest of provocation, I will shelter me here." This was a reference to the supposed aphrodisiac qualities of sweet potatoes and, to a lesser degree, white potatoes, a common belief in Europe at the time the play was written and performed.

Raeann's One Potato– Two Potato Casserole

A very good recipe from a very good friend. Remember this one when you are asked to bring a potato dish to the next big game party. Terrific as a sidekick to sticky ribs or bowls of chili or stew.

MAKES 4 TO 6 SERVINGS

3 large baking potatoes, peeled

3 large sweet potatoes, peeled

Salt

2 green onions, trimmed, finely chopped

1/2 cup (125 mL) butter

1 cup (250 mL) shredded Swiss cheese

1/2 cup (125 mL) shredded old
    Cheddar cheese

1 1/2 tsp (7 mL) salt

Freshly ground pepper

1 1/4 cups (300 mL) whole milk

1 cup (250 mL) fine dry breadcrumbs

1/3 cup (75 mL) grated Parmesan cheese

3 tbsp (45 mL) butter, melted

2 tbsp (30 mL) chopped fresh
    flat-leaf parsley

Cut the baking potatoes and sweet potatoes into chunks of similar size, place the vegetables in separate saucepans, just cover the chunks with cold water and bring to a boil. Add a little salt and cook the vegetables until they are tender, about 20 minutes for the baking potatoes, a little less time for the sweet potatoes. Lightly butter a large (11- x 7-inch/2 L) baking dish. Preheat the oven to 375°F (190°C).

When the potatoes and sweet potatoes are cooked, drain and transfer them both to a single bowl. Use a fork to break up the potatoes slightly (don't mash them). Add the green onions, 1/2 cup (125 mL) butter, Swiss and Cheddar cheeses, salt and pepper. Toss the ingredients gently to combine. Transfer this mixture to the prepared baking dish. Pour the milk over the potato mixture. Combine the breadcrumbs with the Parmesan cheese, melted butter and parsley in a bowl and sprinkle this mixture over the potatoes. Bake the casserole for 20 to 25 minutes, or until hot and crusty brown on the surface. Serve hot.

Index